HOW I BECAME A
PATHFINDER FORCE
NAVIGATOR

1st Edition

Published in 2015 by

Woodfield Publishing Ltd
Bognor Regis PO21 5EL England
www.woodfieldpublishing.co.uk

Copyright © 2015 Peter D. Saville

Cataloguing in Publication Data is available from the British Library

ISBN 1-84683-167-9

Printed and bound in England

Typesetting & page design: Nic Pastorius
Cover design: Klaus Schaffer

(*Source document:* Peter Saville - Pathfinder Force Navigator (final))

How I became a
Pathfinder Force Navigator

*My aircrew training and subsequent
activities with No.35 Squadron RAF
during and after World War Two*

PETER D. SAVILLE

Woodfield Publishing Ltd

Bognor Regis ~ West Sussex ~ England ~ PO21 5EL
tel 01243 821234 ~ e/m info@woodfieldpublishing.co.uk

Interesting and informative books on a variety of subjects

For full details of all our published titles, visit our website at
www.woodfieldpublishing.co.uk

I dedicate this book
to the memory of
my late wife
Barbara.

I acknowledge the assistance
that I have had
from my daughter, Diana,
and my son, Christopher.

Without their help this work
would not have been published.

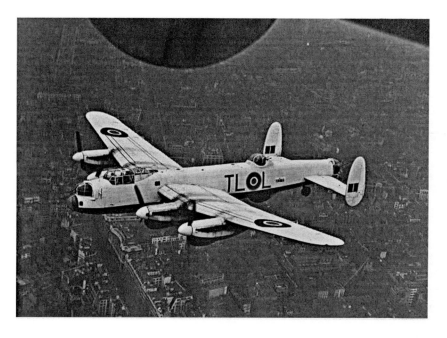

*A 35 Squadron Lancaster in postwar white livery
over London during the Victory Flypast on 8ᵗʰ June 1946.*

Contents

35 Squadron Lancasters over London
during the Victory Flypast on 8ᵗʰ June 1946.
The author was flying in 'E' (centre).

Foreword

Told with quiet modesty, this is the story of one young RAF airman's experiences in war and peace. Too young to join up when the war began in 1939, Peter Saville was one of the thousands of young men from Britain and the Commonwealth who volunteered to join the Royal Air Force (RAF) during World War Two. Inspired by the heroic exploits of The Few during the Battle of Britain, most of these young volunteers dreamed of being fighter pilots, flying solo in a single-engine aircraft and some did indeed achieve this aim, but as the war progressed there arose a greater requirement for aircrew to perform the various roles demanded by the large bomber aircraft now coming into service in large numbers.

An ambitious programme was established to train the thousands of aircrew needed to man the aircraft of RAF Bomber Command. Since airfields in the UK were needed for operational squadrons it was decided that as many aircrew as possible would be trained abroad under the Empire Air Training Scheme.

So it was that Peter set sail from the UK in October 1943 bound for South Africa, where he trained at East London (No.48 Air School) and Port Elizabeth (No.42 Air School) before returning to the UK to finish his training prior to joining an operational squadron.

The unit he was destined to join was No.35 Squadron, one of the five original squadrons of the elite Pathfinder Force (8 Group) founded on Churchill's orders in 1942 to improve the accuracy of RAF bombing raids by marking targets with coloured flares in advance of the main bomber force.

Peter joined this squadron in March 1945, just in time to be involved in some of its last operational sorties of the war when he flew as navigator in bombing raids on Kiel, Bayreuth and Heligoland.

On the 7th May 1945 he navigated an aircraft to the Netherlands in Operation 'Manna', an airdrop of much-needed food and supplies to the starving civilian population – a humanitarian act that the Dutch people still celebrate to this day. On the following day, May 8th, the war in Europe officially ended.

With hostilities over there was still much to be done. No.35 Squadron was among those who participated in Operations 'Exodus' and 'Dodge' – the repatriation of British POWs from Germany and Italy.

Ceremonial duties were also performed in the Victory Flypast over the Netherlands on 4th May 1946 and over London on 8th June 1946.

35 Squadron then had the honour of being selected to represent the RAF on a goodwill tour of the USA, which took place in July/August 1946, a once-in-a-lifetime experience for the 16 Lancaster crews who took part, who flew the Atlantic and were welcomed as honoured guests in New York, Missouri, Colorado, Los Angeles, Texas, Washington DC and Massachusetts.

All this and more is deftly described in this entertaining and eventful memoir.

◆ ◆ ◆

The author is a long time retired Chartered Accountant who practised in The City of London until 1984, Senior Partner of fifteen.

Part I
Aircrew Training

The Air Training Corps crest.

Preface to Part One

I decided to write this story because, as far as I am aware, there is not, nor has there been, any book on the market which chronicles the personal experiences of an airman during his period of training.

During that time I experienced many different situations ranging from the ridiculous to the sublime, from triumph to tragedy, from humour to pathos and from frustration to achievement.

I hope that this story will be read by people of the generations who follow me and that they will be able to appreciate how the training was designed to instil discipline, obedience, enthusiasm, camaraderie and a spirit of pressing on to overcome the problems that would be encountered.

I had been a member of the Air Training Corps where I had earned my Proficiency Certificate so I was not entirely green as were some of those who would train with me.

I have kept no diaries,only a record of the dates spent at the several training establishments, so that most of my subject will be based on memory. For that reason it is possible that some of my memories will be clouded by time but I believe that substantially my account is accurate.

At ITW, June 1943.

~ CHAPTER I ~

The Beginning

I volunteered for aircrew training (pilot, navigator, bomb aimer) in 1942 when I was aged 17½, which was the minimum age at that time. After a short interval I received a letter from the Air Ministry asking me to attend an interview, including aptitude tests, and a medical at Adastral House, Kingsway, London.

I passed the interview and the very strict medical (my Mother was surprised because I had very flat feet and this was usually a cause of rejection). I was told that my dentist would have to examine my teeth and carry out any work that he felt necessary and he would be paid by the Ministry. I was informed that I would receive instructions to report for duty when I was aged 18¼, which was the minimum age that one could be accepted for training in the roles that I had chosen. Shortly after this I received a letter from The Secretary of State for Air, addressed to me as *1814796 AC2 Saville P D*. The content stated that I was now an airman, explained why I would have to wait before I was called up, went on to say that I had been found to be very fit, as one had to be for aircrew, and exhorted me to keep fit during the waiting period.

Early in March 1943 I received notice to report on 22nd March to number 3 Aircrew Reception Centre at Lords Cricket Ground, (ACRC for short, colloquially known as 'Arsy Tarsy'). It was a glorious spring day. There, those of us reporting that day were assembled in flights of thirty (I was to learn that flights of thirty were endemic in the RAF) and we were then marched to our living quarters. The flight that I had joined was taken to a block of luxury flats in Grove Court, where I was allocated a room with three others. I wondered what had happened to the residents when the block had been taken over by the Air Ministry and concluded that the flats had been built just before the war started and had never been residentially occupied. The room contained four beds and furniture for a minimum of clothes. We had pillows and blankets but from memory there were no sheets. Washing and toilet facilities were adjacent.

It was then time to feed us and we were taken to the restaurant in Regents Park Zoo, which had been commandeered. The venue caused some amusement. After lunch we were marched to the clothing store, where we were 'kitted out' with full blue battle dress with forage cap and white flash, greatcoat, waterproof cape, underwear, braces, boots and several pairs of socks. In addition we were issued with physical training kit including plimsolls and standard webbing equipment including a revolver holster but no weapon! All of this was topped up by a kitbag. We were told that Training Command, of which we were now a part, was very insistent that our service clothing should fit well and that if it did not we were to come back to the store and exchange the item or items.

After a wash and brush up, clad in our new uniforms with boots which none of us was used to, we went for our evening meal. We then spent the best part of the first evening trying to make our boots shine, which necessitated a lot of the black polish with which we had been issued and much of our spit. Quite early after a tiring day the four of us took to our beds and we were so tired that we slept well until reveille, which I think was at six am.

After breakfast we had our first formal parade, under the discipline of a Drill Sergeant. The hem of our greatcoats was measured as it had to be a set number of inches from the ground so that all would be uniform. Any that were not so had to be taken to the clothing store to be exchanged. Any airman who was affected by this was told that he must have the greatcoat that he was to receive in exchange measured at the store so that there was no further problem.

The Drill Sergeant then had the unenviable task of turning a group of thirty young men into a unit with a knowledge of efficient drill and marching, and able to put that knowledge into practice. We had been told that we would be at Lords Cricket ground for three weeks before moving on to an Initial Training Wing (ITW) and that at the end of the three weeks we would be expected to be proficient in the work that the Drill Sergeant had taught us.

Later that day we were advised that any of us who lived within reasonable distance of our base, or who had somewhere where they could deposit their civilian clothes, would be given a week-end pass from the coming Saturday morning to the Sunday evening. I took advantage of this. What happened to the clothes of those who were not able to accept the offer, I have no idea.

In the afternoon of that day we were taken to the cinema, where we were joined by airmen of other flights to be shown a film on the horrors of venereal disease. It was not until after the war that I learned that the incidence of V.D. was higher in Bomber Command than in any of the other units in Service. I would imagine that was why we were shown that film, because the majority of us would be destined for

Bomber Command, which at that time was three and a half years in operation from the start of the war. The film was a salutary experience but whether it had the desired effect we would not know.

I think most of us spent that evening doing further work on our boots, which began to show the results of our labours.

Reveille was again at six the following morning and that would be the time every day. We were again put through our drill and marching practice and in the afternoon we were marched to The Seymour Road Baths, where we would swim. Those of us who could swim already were allowed to do so without supervision whilst those who had never previously mastered the art were told in no uncertain terms that they would swim by the end of the three weeks or woe betide.

We were now about half way through the first of the three weeks and were to find that the remainder of that time would be mostly spent drilling, marching and swimming, with just a few hours devoted to talks on subjects on which we would be lectured at ITW and information that we would need to know. We also had inoculations and medical and dental examinations.

At the end of the three weeks we were told to which ITWs we would be going. We had expected that our flight would all be kept together but that was not to be. We were spread around the ITWs, as were the members of the other flights who had finished their three weeks at the same time. I would be going to Number 4, which was at Paignton in South Devon.

The Drill Sergeant, who had been firm but fair and known to use the odd expletive, was pleased with the results that he had achieved as we were quite proficient; not up to Brigade of Guards standard but quite good. Little did we know that at ITW we would be drilled until we matched that standard!

At that time we were not aware that we would be parading in public on such occasions as Wings for Victory.

On the appointed day those of us who were destined for Paignton entrained at Paddington and the next part of our training progamme was about to begin.

With fellow cadets at ITW, June 1943.

~ CHAPTER II ~

№ 4 ITW, Paignton

We duly left the train at Paignton where we were grouped in designated flights of thirty. I was assigned to Flight "C" 3 Squadron where there was a sergeant in charge. He was a former Tottenham Hotspur footballer whom we were to find was a decent chap and very helpful.

Most of the hotels in Paignton had been taken over by the Air Ministry for the duration. Carrying our kitbags on our shoulders, we were marched by the sergeant to the hotels where we were to be accommodated and I found myself in the Ramleh Hotel, in a room on the ground floor with three other airmen who were complete strangers to me. Toilet and washing facilities were next to that room. The beds, we were to find, were comfortable and we had sheets! We were shown how to make our bed to the standard pattern and were warned that if on any morning after we had gone to breakfast a bed was found not to have been made meticulously to that pattern the airman responsible would be for the high jump. The only other furniture in the room was four cabinets for our clothes.

The Ramleh was a small hotel at the western end of the promenade. We would be having our meals at The Palace Hotel which was possibly the largest hotel in the town. It was on the front and about half a mile from the Ramleh. I have no idea how many trainee airmen were based in the town but it must have been a considerable number. The four of us at the Ramleh were very compatible. Three of us were about the same age whilst the other was about thirty. Within quite a short time the older one told us that he would be leaving us within a few days. He was, apparently, a senior civil servant who had been in a reserved occupation. Somehow he had slipped the net to volunteer for aircrew but had been tracked down and recalled. Apparently he was needed to go to Kenya to administer the Groundnut Scheme.

We spent the remainder of that day familiarising ourselves with the area, including The Country Club, where lectures would be held. It was approximately two miles away at the back of the town, where the terrain is quite hilly and the approach would prove to be a rather tiring climb.

The following day we were told what the pattern would be for the duration of our stay of thirteen weeks. So far as was possible the programme for a particular day would be repeated for the ensuing weeks. Each weekday morning after breakfast would be devoted to drill, physical training or

The Ramleh Hotel, Paignton in the 1940s.

sports. After lunch, which would be at a fixed time unless the time needed to be altered because of a cross country run or some other event, we would be marched to The Country Club where we would attend lectures. The subject of these would be airframes, engines – four stroke engine, induction, compression, power and exhaust (that I shall never forget!) theory of flight, aircraft recognition, basic navigation, meteorology, and signals. I think that was all.

At some time during the thirteen weeks examinations would be held on all subjects and it would be essential to achieve a pass, which would be rewarded by promotion to the rank of cadet with an increase in pay to seven shillings and sixpence per day. We had started at ACRC at two shillings and sixpence! There was then, quite an incentive, which was increased by the knowledge that if we did not pass we would be re-mustered to ground staff and that could mean any of the many trades, and it would finish us for aircrew in any role. We were warned that there would be a great deal to learn and that most evenings would have to be devoted to private study.

To break up what would be a busy and tiring week Wednesday afternoons would be devoted to sport when one could choose any one of a number of activities. Some weekends would be partly free, and after church parade on Sundays we would be allowed to go into town or to Torquay. It was a requirement that we were back within bounds by ten thirty both evenings. As a matter of interest, attendance on church parade was compulsory but entering church was left to the choice of the individual if he did not wish to attend the service at that church.

The next day after breakfast we were introduced to the senior physical training instructor (PTI), under whose care we would be for the whole of the course. He was a flight sergeant, aged about thirty and obviously very fit. He was known throughout ITW as Flight Sergeant 'Chang'; I never did discover his real name.[1] He was a great character.

He had a chart in his office to record the progress of each flight. At the bottom of the chart was the inscription "W*****s d**m". The emphasis was on team work and depending upon the number of points scored on each task the flight would climb the chart until it reached the top which was "Members of the Temple of the illustrious Chang".

I felt that this was a good idea, as it instilled interest.

He told us that if we thought we were fit he would make jolly sure that we actually would be by the end of the course.

The following morning we met our drill instructor, another Flight Sergeant. He was a foul mouthed bully; almost every instruction contained an expletive such as "Swing your b*****y arms to shoulder height" or "have you got two f*****g left feet?" or "hold your b****y head up or I'll come over and p**s in your optic". Nevertheless he drilled us to a very high standard by the end of the course.

I am reminded of an amusing incident. One of our number, let us call him Brown, professed to have a stammer. If one was addressed by an instructor, simply as airman the response was, in my case, Saville 796 followed by the instructor's rank. Always one's full name and the last three of one's full number. Brown was addressed and his response was "b-b-b-Brown 455556 Flight Sergeant". I cannot believe that he had a stammer because if that was the case I doubt whether he would have passed his medical. I think he was putting it on as a bit of a lark. The Flight Sergeant asked him to repeat his

---

[1] Editor's note: according to another former airman's memoir (published on a BBC website) Flight Sergeant Chang's surname was Warner.

name and last three, which he then did without the stammer. He did not try this too often but it caused a little amusement among the rest of us.

The next day , which must have been Thursday, we were told after breakfast that we were to go on a cross-country run that morning under the care of Chang and that we were to be ready, kitted out in PT kit and plimsolls, at 9am.

Headed by Chang, who kept quiet after telling us that we were to do as he said without variation, we set off in a westerly direction. A little way along the road was a stationary truck. Chang crawled underneath. With some trepidation we all followed. Some way ahead was the promenade. When we reached there, Chang jumped down several feet to the sand, with us not far behind. Scrambling over the pier supports was the next obstacle and so it went on as we attacked the course. I cannot remember how far we ran on that first occasion. Most of us were almost 'all in' by the time we finished but, to the credit of the flight, we had kept going, as we were determined to climb that ladder. Chang told us that we had done quite well for the first run and he would consider moving us up one rung of the ladder. This we found he had done when we next had occasion to look at it. I think we all felt that those cross-country runs would not get any easier and would probably become increasingly difficult. How right we would be proved to be!

The afternoon of the Wednesday of the following week was our first experience of a choice of sports. I decided to try horse-riding, of which I had no experience whatever. I was assisted on to the horse which had looked to me to be quite big. I was told how to control the beast with the reins and a few words and how to get us on our way. The horse took about five steps and then threw me! Fortunately, I landed on soft grass and was unhurt apart from a few bruises. I have never ventured to ride a horse again from that day to this.

Thinking about this incident some time later, I cynically wondered if the horse had been trained to do this as part of the process of toughening up the young aircrew aspirants but, rightly or wrongly, I concluded that it would have been too dangerous to continue my equestrian endeavours.

On another occasion we were introduced by Chang to a game to which he had given some thought and which he had named 'Changball'. It was really a glorified form of Rugby played by one half of a flight, that is fifteen players. There were no holds barred except that one was not allowed to kick an opponent in the groin where it hurt most but that, of course, did not stop it happening when the referee's attention was elsewhere. At the time that I was at Paignton there was a flight of thirty airmen from Czechoslovakia who had somehow eluded the Nazis and fled to England. They were tough (they *really* were tough) and it was said that they won all their games of Changball.

You will have gathered that we had little time for leisure of our choice but there were two aspects of this that I particularly remember. In the town there was a department store by the name of Dellars, which had a restaurant and a dance floor. On most Saturday evenings there was a dance and many of us would go there to dance with the local girls.

As something completely different, one of our number had discovered a small café near the pier where he said they served baked beans on fried bread. A few of us went with him one evening and from then on we were regular customers when the café was open. As a change from our daily food, which actually was quite good and nutritious for wartime food, the bread fried in beef dripping (where the beef came from, I know not) and topped with baked beans was delicious.

I thoroughly enjoyed my time at Paignton, which was a pleasant resort on the south Devon coast. The weather was very good; I cannot remember rain the whole time we were there. We were a good flight and I believe most of us passed the exams and received our promotion. We also reached the top of Chang's chart.

On the 30th July we were told that we would be leaving Paignton the next day bound for an Elementary Flying Training School (EFTS) to begin our pilot training. I would be off to 22 EFTS at Cambridge. Once again our flight was split up to attend EFTSs all over the UK and not one of my former colleagues was to come to Cambridge.

◆ ◆ ◆

~ CHAPTER III ~

№ 22 EFTS Cambridge

Cambridge EFTS was on the site of the local Flying Club, owned by Marshalls, and at the time of writing is now a flourishing local airport. In 1943 it was a grass airfield on which were to be found a number of De Havilland Tiger Moth (DH82A) biplanes. On that occasion only a few of us had come to Cambridge from ITW. We were comfortably accommodated and the food was up to the quality of that at Paignton. We were told that we would have eight hours dual instruction after which the Chief Flying Instructor (CFI) would judge whether we were competent to go solo (an exciting prospect).

The weather the following day was perfect for flying and would remain so whilst we were there. I met my instructor who was a flight lieutenant, former fighter pilot who had been decorated with a Distinguished Flying Cross (DFC). He was a very nice chap and so patient. We walked around his Tiger Moth and he explained to me the function of the flaps and rudder, etc, which, of course, we had previously been taught at ITW, and how essential it was to do a pre-flight check. We then climbed into the Moth, he in the rear seat and me in the front.

The position and function of the controls was explained to me and the start-up procedure, which would involve a mechanic swinging the prop. My instructor said that it was vital from that point onwards that I did exactly as he told me without any change, however slight. The mechanic swung the prop, the engine fired and shortly after we were given the signal to take off. What a thrill!

In the ATC I had experienced two flights, the first in a Tiger Moth at North Weald and the second in a Fairey Fulmar at Yeovilton, so I was not entirely green. In this first flight of my pilot training I was shown how to pull the control column towards me and to control the power with the knob the right side of me, and the other controls the function of which had previously been explained to me at ITW, as we made a gentle climb to about 1,000 feet. We were to do a circuit of the airfield at that height, involving a number of turns, which I was shown how to execute.

As we approached the end of the hour, the instructor said that a good landing was possibly the most difficult task to master at this stage of the eight hours and at this early stage I was to hand over the controls to him for the landing. When we came to a halt after a perfect landing he told me what we had to do before we left the plane. He also said that I had done reasonably well in my first hour of instruction.

The general atmosphere at Cambridge was quite relaxed compared with Paignton. I think this may have been deliberate because most of us were tackling something that was completely new to us and understandably our nervous systems were reacting.

The time went quickly by. We flew about every third day with most of us absorbing the fine instruction and becoming more proficient. However, in my case, whilst I had mastered everything else to a good standard, I could not judge the landing. I would either bang down the Moth on to the grass or try to land several feet above. Towards the end of the final of the eight hours, the CFI took the dual control and at the end he said, "I cannot permit you to go solo. Whilst you are generally up to minimum standard you cannot land the bloody thing!"

I was bitterly disappointed because I knew that his decision meant that I had no future as a pilot and would have to re-muster for the role of trainee navigator/bomb aimer.

There was one incident at Cambridge which I recall. The centre of the upper main plane of a Tiger Moth is the petrol tank. One day whilst I was waiting my turn for instruction there was a cadet about to take off on his first solo. As he opened the throttle the tank detached and hit him on the head. Fortunately, he managed to move the throttle lever back to off and the Moth came to a halt. The cadet was not hurt to any degree but that accident could have proved fatal. No doubt the mechanic who had serviced the plane would be put on a serious charge. And what had happened to the pre-flight check?

The day after I failed my solo I was told that I had fourteen days leave and was to report to RAF Heaton Park, Manchester on 14th September. Heaton Park was a holding centre for trainee aircrew awaiting posting for further training, from where we would most probably go overseas under The Empire Air Training Scheme.

◆ ◆ ◆

CHAPTER IV

RAF Heaton Park, Manchester

O ne memory from that leave. I went to see my father, who was convalescing after an operation. After the war ended he told me that his foremost thought during that visit had been that he might never see me again. I mention this because most of the time I gave no thought to what my parents might be thinking during the time I was away and I feel sure I was not alone in what was a selfish attitude.

When I arrived at Heaton Park on that day in September it was raining. The Park looked rather dreary. I was to be in 2 Squadron, accommodated in Hut 65. For nine days our squadron was drilled, given physical training and fed. There was little else. Discipline was tight.

Then, on 20th September, a number of us were attached to B Squadron, 2 Wing, RAF Weeton for agricultural work, which we were to do for two weeks. It consisted of harvesting potatoes, which was back-breaking work. I have few memories of Weeton which perhaps was because nothing much happened. I remember on one occasion sheltering in a barn whilst it was raining and watching the birth of a calf which was another experience. We were allowed off base on the middle Sunday and some of us paid a visit to Blackpool.

On 4th October we returned to Heaton Park and were told that because there was no empty accommodation we would be billeted in houses in Salford, a tram ride from the Park.

My abode was to be a dingy small terraced house, almost a slum. The landlady had let one room to the Ministry or most likely it had been requisitioned. Four of us slept in that room in very cramped conditions. There was no furniture other than the four beds and nowhere to put one's clothes so we lived out of our kit bags and piled our clothes on top when we went to bed. There were no washing or toilet facilities so it was an early rise to catch the first tram to the Park. We had to remember to take with us everything that we would require that day as there was no question of a return before the evening. It was a miserable existence and one of my worst experiences in the Service but fortunately it did not last very long.

Shortly before that time came to an end we were issued with a new kit bag and were told to stencil the letters SCSC thereon. This was obviously the code for our destination but no-one had a clue as to where this would be. We were told that everything that we were to take with us would have to go in that bag except for small items in our webbing haversack. We would not be permitted to carry anything else whatsoever. The rumour was that we would be moving out the next evening.

Rumours are often proved to be what happens. That evening we piled onto trucks and were taken to one of the Manchester stations, where we entrained and all had a seat (very unusual in wartime). I slept through the night and awoke at dawn, just as the train was steaming into a docks area. It turned out to be Gourock, on the Clyde. Alongside the dock was MV *Tegelburg,* which we would be boarding later that day but we still had no idea where we would be going. Our address until further notice was SCSC RAF c/o APO 4975.

~ CHAPTER V ~

Outward Bound

MV *Tegelberg* was a modern Dutch registered freighter of some 15,000 tons, presumably chartered to the Air Ministry for conversion to a troopship. The holds below the main deck had been converted into accommodation of sorts where the occupants would eat, sleep in hammocks and "live" for some time. The hold to which I was directed was to accommodate 140 men. Sleeping in a hammock would be another new experience for the majority of us.

We left the dock the next morning and sailed from the Clyde south through the Irish Sea and St George's Channel to the Atlantic. There we joined a large convoy, very large indeed. I have no idea how many ships there were but it was rumoured that we were to have an escort of twenty destroyers, so it must have been a convoy of some importance.

It was all rather exciting but we still did not know where we were bound. However, it seemed unlikely that a convoy of that size would be heading for the eastern seaboard of Canada or the United States, as we had heard that it was the big liners, the *Queen Mary* and *Queen Elizabeth* and the like which crossed the Atlantic unescorted because of their speed.

I doubt that many of us realized the dangers we would be facing. I for one did not.

The convoy duly moved off and we headed south. This reinforced our opinion that we must be on our way to South

MV Tegelburg.

Africa or Rhodesia and we prepared ourselves for a long voyage down the West Coast of Africa to dock at either Cape Town or Durban.

Apart from daily physical training exercises we had nothing organized for us on board; there was no place where lectures could be given and if there had been there appeared to be no-one competent to deliver them, so our time was spent either on deck looking at a few ships of the convoy or perhaps a glimpse of one of the escorts or somewhere on deck, reading, writing letters or playing cards. There was a place on the deck where there was a small shop but on this voyage it stocked only tins of condensed milk. We used to buy this and have it with ship's biscuits. If these were tapped on to the table, weevils ran out! I cannot remember what the food was like but we had to fetch this from the galley on a roster basis. We then helped ourselves using the metal plates provided, which afterwards we had to wash, together with the 'irons' (knife fork and spoon) with which we had been issued at ACRC.

The 'heads' and washing facilities were adequate.

All went reasonably well until we entered the Bay of Biscay. October is the worst time of year to go through Biscay as the sea tends to be rather rough. It really was rough for some days. Everyone on our deck was seasick apart from me and one other and the mess was indescribable. However, we cleaned it up and after the seas were calmer the problem was soon forgotten.

We then proceeded down the west coast of Portugal and Spain until some days later we were surprised when the convoy turned to port and we guessed that we would be going through The Straits of Gibraltar into the Mediterranean. The reason for the size of the convoy then became clear. It was mainly to supply and reinforce the Eighth Army (which was then fighting its way through Italy) with food, arms, munitions, etc, and possibly more troops. Security had been very tight.

The Rock was an awesome sight. It would be the first time that the majority of us had seen it and I suppose that for most of us it would be the first time that we had been out of the UK.

The following evening, at dusk and without any warning, the convoy was dive-bombed by German Stukas. The swastikas on the airframes stood out in the sunset. The voice of the Dutch Captain came calmly over the Tannoy. "Everyone below deck." There we waited, with the sound of bombs bursting around us, until after about thirty minutes we were given the all clear to go back on deck. We had been so fortunate. We had lost only one man, an RAF military policeman, who had been struck by a piece of shrapnel as he was shepherding men below. The convoy had, of course, scattered and it seems incredible that we never saw another ship during the remainder of that voyage, which was to terminate at Port Said. Rumour had it that the convoy had been decimated, including a ship carrying WRNS destined for Cairo and none had survived. How true this was, I do not know.

The rest of that voyage was very peaceful. We witnessed glorious sunsets, saw flying fishes and other birds indigenous to that part of the world and at times had glimpses of the North African coast.

It must have been about three weeks after we left Gourock that we docked at Port Said, where there was so much activity. We were taken to a tented encampment from where, after a few days, we went by truck to Port Suez, at the northern end of The Canal, where we boarded a train to be taken along the western banks of The Canal to the southern end, Port Tewfik, where we were to board the *Empire Trooper* for the voyage to Durban.

Typing this part of the story has brought home to me the logistical task of moving us first around the UK and then by ship and train to the end of the Suez Canal. We were just one small part of an enormous body of men and women who were constantly on the move and there must have been remarkable feats of organization.

The *Empire Trooper* was an old, decrepit, dirty, rusty former freighter, or so I would guess. It had probably been converted in the thirties to transport troops to India. It was British registered and was of about the same tonnage as the *Tegelburg* but that was its only similarity. I do not remember how many were accommodated on the deck where I was, but it was a large number. The 'heads' and the washing facilities were inadequate. The standard of hygiene was low and it was not long before dysentery broke out.

We set sail through the Red Sea, the Gulf of Aden and into the Indian Ocean. The speed of a convoy is that of the slowest ship and the convoy plodded on at seven knots. It was a small convoy and we had only two escort ships. On we went, along the east coast of Africa, the weather was clear but it was hot and the strength of this increased as we went through the tropics towards the Equator, which we duly crossed. There was no ceremony. There was very little shade on the ship, no air conditioning and the heat below decks was almost unbearable. We eventually arrived at Durban on 10th December 1943. We were late because of the troubles that we had had in the Med and the slowness of the second convoy. Many of the chaps were tired, others were unwell because of the effects of dysentery and I would think that most of us had lost weight because of the heat on that ship.

There was a train at the dockside awaiting our arrival. We boarded and were soon on our way to 48 Air School East London. The South African Railways were "built on the cheap" insofar as instead of tunneling through the hills and mountains the engineers went round them. In consequence if one was in the observation car at the back of the train quite often one would see the engine apparently on a parallel track going in the opposite direction. South Africa is a vast country as compared to the UK and the distances between towns are considerable. The journey to East London took three days and two nights with stops for meals. It was another memorable experience as we passed through some beautiful and wonderful scenery.

◆ ◆ ◆

~ CHAPTER VI ~

№ 48 Air School, East London, South Africa

The Air School was, somewhat paradoxically, a ground school at Woodbrook, a suburb of East London. We were welcomed by the adjutant who told us that our late arrival had disrupted the training programme; the time for the journey from the UK had previously been six weeks (presumably the west coast route) and we had taken eight through no fault of ours. He asked us to co-operate to help to get the timetable back on schedule. He told us what he felt we would need to know about The Union and in particular to observe the laws on apartheid. He suggested it would be helpful if we tried to master Afrikaans, the official language, but he doubted we would be able to do this as the course was intensive and we would have little time to learn something else. He also warned us about the OB, a pro-German organization which had freedom of speech and movement in The Union.

We were accommodated in huts with two-tier bunks and were grouped in flights of thirty men. The beds were comfortable and we had sheets. The weather was glorious, it was the height of summer, the food was good and we were to find that the hospitality of the East Londoners was wonderful. After the privations that we had suffered in the past months I think we all felt very happy. It was nearly Christmas and I remember spending Boxing Day on the beach with a picnic provided by the community. Soon after the festivities a colleague and I were introduced to a couple who owned a department store in the town. The couple were obviously quite well off, which was evident from the house at which we stayed on occasions. They were so very kind to us. We were invited by them to lunch, sometimes on a Sunday, and we would then go for a drive in his Packard automobile. On Saturdays we often went to a dance, usually at the YWCA. I became friendly with a girl who lived elsewhere in South Africa but worked in East London and lodged at the YWCA.

Discipline at The Air School was pretty strict but somewhat surprisingly it did not extend to wearing service issue khaki drill, which was pretty awful, so some of us bought new shorts and shirts and had our service shorts shortened.

The plan at the Air School was to give us a thorough ground training in all the subjects that we would be putting into practice in the air at the next school if we passed the exams at the end of the course in East London. Those subjects comprised Dead Reckoning and Astro Navigation, Meteorology, Signals (including Morse Code) Aircraft Recognition and one or two minor subjects. The course was intensive and there was the incentive that if we did not pass the future would be bleak indeed, we might go anywhere but back to the UK would be most unlikely.

The instructors were very good. Towards the end of the course the exams were held and those of us who had passed were handed our "Observers and Air Gunner's Flying Log Book" and we were each given our results on a slip of paper to paste in. Mine read: *Pass, 75%. Very efficient. Just above average.* I was so pleased. In a few days those of us who had passed would be off to the Air School, which this time would not belie its name and where, if we successfully completed the course, we would graduate as Navigators and be awarded our brevets.

The Observer's and Air Gunner's Log Book was a product of The South African Air Force. Unfortunately, because it was wartime the paper was of poor quality and would react to some inks like blotting paper.

With fellow cadets on the course at No.48 Air School East London.

CHAPTER VII

№ 42 Air School, Port Elizabeth, South Africa

We arrived at the Air School on 18th March 1944. The School was similar in design to the one at East London with the addition of an airfield on which there were a number of Avro Anson twin-engine monoplanes. They were flown by pilots of the South African Air Force who were lieutenants (they had Army ranks in the SAAF) all of whom had flown on operations in the Middle East, some of them having been decorated. We were to find that, quite understandably, they were a bit cheesed off after operational flying at having to stooge around the skies of South Africa flying trainee navigators on their navigation exercises. It would be found to be quite embarrassing to have to say "Sir, would you please fly the course I have given you? We have gone off track, which will make a mockery of my chart." Usually with good humour they would do as requested. They were a grand bunch, not much older than most of us. At times, to relieve their boredom, they would play hide and seek in the cumulus clouds. Exciting and dangerous but we loved it.

Our accommodation and the Mess was similar to that of the previous school. We had comfortable two-tier bunks once again and the quality and quantity of the food was very good. There were no shortages in wartime South Africa.

We attended ground school and on average once every two days we would fly our navigation exercises, sometimes at night. Each trip was for two or three hours, sometimes four, mostly over the Indian Ocean by day and over land by night. On each flight the Anson would carry two trainee navigators, the *first nav* to do the plotting whilst the *second nav* map read, took astro shots of the sun by day and the stars by night, drifts off the sea and wireless bearings, all of which he reported to the first nav to plot. On my first flight a colleague was first nav and I was second. We had no sooner taken off than the first nav was violently air sick. I took over the plot and wrote in the log, "First navigator airsick, second navigator taking over". That showed initiative and was a feather in my cap.

We completed the exercise and I made the first entry in my flying log book: *22 March 1944. 13.20 Lt Winn 1 hour.*

I was on my way.

Later that month I was flying as first nav and duly handed in my log when we landed. Some little while later I was told to report to the office of the Chief Navigation Instructor. He had my log in his hand.

"Saville, you did not write this log in the air," he said.

I was rather taken aback. "I did sir."

"I don't believe you, it's too neat."

"I can only repeat that I did sir."

"I'm coming with you next time to watch you work."

This he did – and had the good grace to apologise and to say, "I am having your log copied and sent to the other Air Schools as an example of how it is possible to keep a log in the air."

That was another plus mark for me.

On a later trip we had to look out for Japanese submarines, which had been detected quite close to the coast in the vicinity of Port Elisabeth. This was officially described as an *anti-sub patrol*. I enquired what we were to do if any were sighted. I was told to advise the pilot, who may probably have seen them, and he would contact base to report the matter. That was a trip of four hours, which was my longest while at the school.

I flew for the final time at 42 Air School on 26th June 1944, having flown a total of 73.25 hours by day and 31.55 hours by night, the total of which involved 41 take-offs and landings. I had really enjoyed that wonderful experience. Not much had happened as we flew over the Indian Ocean but it was on those trips that we concentrated on our plot with the aim of sighting land at the point we had aimed for and for this we needed the co-operation of the pilots to fly the course that we had given them as I have written earlier. Because most of the flights over land were by night we saw little of the landscape of South Africa but what we did see was quite awesome.

During the first week at the school I was near the front of the queue for the NAAFI wagon at mid-morning break when I noticed a South African Air Force WAAF about to join the long queue. I beckoned her over and asked if I could get her something. We found a seat and enjoyed our break together. Such was South African hospitality that she asked if I would care to visit her house, meet her Mum and have lunch with them the next Sunday. Of course I accepted. The following Saturday we were confined to camp for the weekend because our hut was not clean enough. I was furious, there was no way that I could contact my new friend, I had no address nor telephone number. The following Monday as soon as I had the opportunity I found her and apologised. She quite understood and said we should make it the next weekend, which we did. From then on we became very close and spent much of our spare time together. She accepted that I was having to study hard, so we met only at the weekends. She was good company and great fun. She was an anglicised South African who lived with her mother in a suburb of the town.

She was a very attractive girl and we had some good times together but later, when I had time to reflect, I think her plan may have been to marry an airman and get to the UK, but perhaps I misjudged her.

We were due to graduate on 1ˢᵗ July. On the previous evening I was sent for by the Station Adjutant who told me that I had passed the course and would graduate the next day. My marks averaged 74.5% for my groundwork and 71.2% for my work in the air. The remarks were: *Practical astro assessment above average. Weak Met. Recommended for specialist training in navigation after further experience.* The adjutant then told me that I would be commissioned at the passing out parade as a Pilot Officer. I was ecstatic, one of only three on our course of thirty. After my disappointment at EFTS I was determined that I would qualify as a navigator but in my wildest dreams it had never occurred to me that I might be commissioned.

At the graduation ceremony the next day I was handed my navigator's brevet and my Pilot Officer's ribbon which my girlfriend later sewed on to my battledress prior to a small party that she had laid on for me that evening.

I sent a telegram home to tell them of my achievements. My life in The Royal Air Force was to change dramatically from then on. I was an officer. I would be living in and dining in the Mess. I would be travelling first class. I would be respected (a respect that I first had to earn) and I would have responsibilities.

We left Port Elizabeth the next day and I bid a fond farewell to my girlfriend, who I would never see again. We were bound for Durban, which was about 600 miles from Port Elizabeth by rail, so there was a long journey ahead.

◆ ◆ ◆

Graduation day at No.42 Air School, Port Elizabeth.

~ CHAPTER VIII ~

RAF Transit Camp, Durban, South Africa

This was a camp for newly-qualified aircrew who would either be sent to the Middle East or, if they were fortunate, back to the UK. Exceptionally, they could be destined for the Far East. We had a nice Mess in which to eat and relax and pleasant quarters in which to sleep. Many newly-commissioned officers could not wait to have a suit of best blue made and I was one of those. There was an Indian tailor on the camp who was a rogue but that was not known to me. I asked him to make me a suit and a greatcoat. He was crafty. He would somehow get to know when his customer would be leaving camp for good and would produce the order the evening before, when it was too late to have any alterations made. My suit was too tight and my greatcoat an abomination. I had asked him several times why there was a delay in the making and there was always an excuse.

However, quite a lot was to happen before he handed the order to me. For some reason neither he nor the stores were able to provide the standard badge for the peaked cap and we had to make do with a very inferior alternative.

There was little for us to do and after the problems and the hard work that had preceded it, life was very easy. However, I was pleased to be told that I would be escorting a new intake to East London. This would be the first test of my new responsibilities. The intake comprised thirty ex-policemen, aged about thirty, who had been deferred from aircrew training because they were in a reserved occupation. I was nineteen and was, at first, rather apprehensive. I felt somewhat self-conscious but that I soon overcame. In the event the cadets behaved themselves and I had no problems. On the train I had a first class compartment with a comfortable bed and washing facilities and all my meals were brought to me. I duly delivered the intake to the Air School and was able to spend one night with my friends before catching the train back to Durban.

Whilst at the camp one had to be duty officer on a rota basis. The principal task was to be available throughout one's tour of duty of twenty four hours to alert aircrew who would be leaving the camp the next day. There was a pilot with whom I had become friendly who had a girl in town. He was due to be duty officer on a particular day and asked me if I would swap the duty with him as he wanted to see his girl to say goodbye and was doubtful if he would ever see her again if he was unable to see her on that day. We exchanged duties but unfortunately he omitted to tell the Admin Section, with the result that those who should have been alerted during the night were not called. There was, of course, a hell of a row about this and we were both in trouble. However, I escaped any form of punishment as it had been no fault of mine.

I had acquired rather a lot of clothes during my stay in the Union, so I bought a large valise in Durban to take the place of my kit bag. I decided to take home tinned food, which was unobtainable in the UK in wartime. I acquired a strong wooden box large enough to contain my purchases. I had access to the workshops on the camp where I painted the box a dark brown and wrote my rank and name in white when the brown paint was dry. I nailed down the lid and roped the box including a handle with which to carry it. To accompany me on my further travels I now had the valise and the box, an overnight bag and my greatcoat and thought I could just about manage that lot.

After about a month in Durban I was told that I would be returning to the UK and was to be ready the following morning to catch a train to Cape Town Dock, where I was to board MV *Louis Pasteur* for the homeward voyage. Cape Town is more than 1,000 miles from Durban, so it was going to be a very long journey. I have no recollection of that trip and no record of the date on which I arrived in Cape Town. There was no chance to look around, it was a case of 'off the train and onto the ship'.

◆ ◆ ◆

Newly qualified, with Navigator's brevet proudly on display.

~ CHAPTER IX ~

Homeward Bound

The *Louis Pasteur* was a ship of between 15 and 20 thousand tons, I would think. I was told that it was under construction in France at the time of Dunkirk and that apparently we nipped over the Channel, collared it and brought it back to the UK, where it was finished off on the Clyde. Being quite new, it was equipped with the latest marine technology. It was American provisioned, from which I gathered it had been on the trooping run in preparation for "D- Day". Again, the privileges of an officer, I had a luxury cabin to myself. The officers had three substantial meals of excellent quality each day with a printed menu at each meal. In stark contrast, those with whom I had trained and had not been commissioned but had been promoted to Sergeant if they had passed the course were manning the anti-aircraft guns, amongst other duties. It was a fast ship. We averaged 29 knots by day and 22 by night. Because of the speed we were unescorted and reached Liverpool fourteen days after leaving Cape Town, which must have been something of a record.

As was the case at Durban, there was a rota for duty officer. We had 3,000 Italian prisoners of war on board, who were quartered in the bowels of the ship, in what I considered were dreadful conditions. It was the job of the duty officer to have those prisoners counted every evening, to what purpose defeated me as they could not have gone far in the

Atlantic, but perhaps it was felt that they could have escaped from where they were confined and stowed away until we reached land. It soon became clear to me that no officer had bothered about the count since we had left dock but, being newly commissioned and keen to obey the rules, I decided to do the count. It was reported to me that the total count came to 3001! I then had to order a check against the list of names on the ship's manifest, not an easy job because of the Italian names but, fortunately, one of their number spoke fluent English and he was a great help. He was a cultured man and I felt sorry for him in those conditions. We did have 3001, which meant that a mistake had been made before they had left the POW compound.

We had no more untoward incidents and we docked in Liverpool in August 1944. We were sent on leave and I had instructions to report to RAF Harrogate on 25th August. I struggled home with my load of things and eventually reached there, to be greeted by my parents, who were so happy and thankful that up to that point I had emerged unscathed. Mother insisted that one of the first things I must do was to visit a professional photographer and have a head and shoulders shot, which I did the next day. I do not remember much of that leave except that I went dancing with my former girlfriend before I went to South Africa. We decided that we did not have much in common and that was the final time that I saw her.

◆ ◆ ◆

~ CHAPTER X ~

RAF Harrogate, England

I duly reported to RAF Harrogate on 25th August and was allocated a room, which I would share with four other newly-qualified officers, in The Queens Hotel which, prior to the war, had been one of the resort's first class hotels.

There were so many newly-qualified pilot and navigator officers that the Air Ministry was at a loss to know what to do with them. The Ministry's problem was exacerbated by the number of newly qualified sergeants, who were in a similar transit camp elsewhere. The problem had arisen because the aircrew losses since D-Day had been less than anticipated and there were far too many newcomers to cope with. The authorities were very concerned that, after months of hard training, these newly-qualified pilots and navigators had reached a peak and the danger was that they would soon become stale. Lectures were arranged in an endeavour to hold our interest and sports and physical training sessions were instituted with a view to retaining our fitness.

I had corresponded with Barbara, one of my former girlfriends, whilst I was in South Africa and had let her know that I was back in the UK. She had moved with her parents to West Bridgford, just outside Nottingham. She had told her mother that I was at Harrogate and her mother had said that if I was anywhere near Nottingham she and Barbara's father would be pleased to see me and hear of my experiences in South Africa, as Barbara's brother Tony had qualified as a pilot in Rhodesia and was to stay out there for a while as an instructor. I telephoned Barbara and said that I would come the next weekend, if that was convenient. I think Barbara's mother was a little taken aback but she said, "Yes, I would be very welcome." I had a very pleasant weekend at West Bridgford and was made most welcome. That was to be the beginning of my courtship of Barbara, which led to our marriage in March 1947.

Back at Harrogate after that weekend, I met up with an old friend from Chingford. He had qualified in Canada as a pilot and, like me, was awaiting a posting. We had some good times together. He had a grandmother who lived at Knaresborough, which is not far from Harrogate, and we quite often went to have tea with her on a Sunday afternoon. It was not until some years later that Barbara told me that my friend had hoped that he might marry Barbara one day and was disappointed when he found that Barbara and I were close. In a way I think it rather strange the way in which the crowd of friends at Chingford (from the ATC days) were paired off. My friend married another one of the girls, and I suppose it could have happened the other way around, but the important thing is that all the marriages lasted, at least as far as I am aware from the contacts that I still have.

The normal progression from Harrogate for a navigator would be a posting to Advanced Flying Unit (AFU) and thence to Operational Training Unit (OTU), to be crewed up before the whole crew was posted to a Conversion Unit (CU) before joining a squadron. In an attempt to deal with the number of new aircrew at Harrogate, the Air Ministry cooked up a Pre-AFU, which meant both the pilots and navigators going back to an EFTS, where they would fly navigation map-reading exercises in Tiger Moths. I found myself posted to Perth in Scotland and I reckoned it would be ages before I was able to see Barbara again. Quite by chance I had become friendly in the Mess with the Unit's Movements Officer and I asked him if he could switch me with someone who had been posted to Cambridge. He said he would try. He was as good as his word and off I went to Cambridge. On the train I found that I appeared to be the only navigator! I wondered if the Movements Officer had made a mistake and I was going to be rather busy. I need not have worried. We were joined at Cambridge by sergeant navigators from the other transit camp.

◆ ◆ ◆

CHAPTER XI

№ 22 EFTS, Cambridge

This should have been familiar territory but no, I was sent to the satellite grass airfield at Caxton Gibbet, north of Cambridge. It was rumoured that Dick Turpin had been hanged at The Gibbet, but I found later this was carried out at York. However, it would appear that he had been often in the vicinity. The discipline at the grass field was very relaxed. There were probably less than twenty of us and unusually the officers, NCOs and airmen shared the same Mess. It would have been impracticable to have had the normal arrangements.

The weather was poor but for the first few days we were able to fly short map-reading exercises. The weather then clamped down and we were unable to fly for some days until towards the end of December it was decided that conditions were such that we could undertake a map-reading exercise of about 150 miles, three legs each of 50 miles in the form of a triangle. We took off, it started to rain, the visibility was poor and we really should have aborted the exercise. We climbed to our operating height of 1,000 feet and shortly after, to my horror, I found that we had flown off the sheet of the map that I had brought with me! My pilot was a New Zealand sergeant who had not previously flown in this country but that was irrelevant; he was there to fly the courses that I gave him. To this day I have no idea what had gone wrong. Perhaps he had flown a course other than the one that I had given him but that was no excuse, as I had a repeater compass and I should have checked.

He sensed that something was wrong and said, "Do you know where we are, Sir?"

I said "No" and explained what had happened. To his credit his reply was, "Then we had better find out".

At that time there was a considerable number of bomber airfields in East Anglia, both RAF and USAAF. We found an American airfield, which turned out to be Polebrook. We landed unannounced and taxied to the Control Tower. I got out and climbed the steps to the Control Room, which was empty apart from a young American lieutenant, who welcomed me and asked me what he could do for me. He was so relaxed, it was just as if he was regularly confronted by a lost RAF navigator. Perhaps he was! I rather unnecessarily and embarrassingly told him that my pilot and I were lost.

After telling him where we were bound, we looked at the map and he showed me the way. What this boiled down to was to follow the east coast railway line. He asked me to hurry to get the hell out of there, as there was a squadron of Liberators returning from a raid and they would not be best pleased to be held up by a Tiger Moth. I thanked him, went back to the Moth and told the pilot. He asked me if I had ever started one of these. I replied that I had not. He told me to get two lumps of concrete or large stones and place them under the front of the wheels. On these hastily-built wartime airfields there were usually lumps of concrete lying around so that was no problem.

"When I give the word, swing the prop and we'll hope the engine fires," he said.

It did, and we taxied towards the runway. The Moth does not have a tailwheel, it has a skid. I was concerned that we appeared to be dragging up cables which ran from the Control Tower to the caravan at the end of the runway. Another black mark. I just hoped that we had not damaged the cables. We took off across the runway, flew parallel to it, turned to starboard at the end, found the railway line and were soon back at the Gibbet. On the way back I had a vision of the entry in my log book recommending specialist navigation duties after further experience and wondered if this incident would damn me. We reported to the senior officer and, rather remarkably, we never heard another word. It was fortunate that my pilot had chosen a USAAF airfield. Had it been RAF I doubt that it would have had such a happy ending. The Yanks were very relaxed about that sort of thing, as I was to have confirmed at a later time.

That was the final time that I flew from the Gibbet, as I was told later that day that I was posted to No 4 AFU(O) at West Freugh on the west coast of Scotland and that I would be making the journey, in the company of others, the following day.

◆ ◆ ◆

~ CHAPTER XII ~

№ 4 AFU(O) West Freugh, Scotland

W e left the train at Stranraer Station on 1st January 1945 and were taken by road to the base. We passed through the village from which the base had taken its name. It appeared to be a damp and dreary place but that, no doubt, was because of the time of year and the weather. The fact that it was an important day in the Scots calendar seemed to make no difference! That would be the only time that I would have a glimpse of that village.

The base was a typical wartime construction of Nissen huts and, like the village, appeared to be a depressing place. We had intensive ground training in advanced navigation and did not fly until half way through the month. The aircraft were Avro Ansons, similar to the ones in which we had flown in South Africa. They were flown by staff pilots but I did not learn anything of their background. My first flight was in daylight over the west coast. The route was from base to Barra, Scalasaig, Coloraine and back to base. The duration was three hours forty minutes and was at a height of 5,000 feet. The next flight was again over the west coast and the Isles, but a different route. After a gap of almost a week I flew at night for the first time, over the local area, identifying night visual aids. That same night I flew from base to Tiree, Chicken's Rock and back to base, which lasted three hours. There followed two further night flights over the west coast and the Isles, the first at 4,000 feet and the second at 6,000. That would be my final flight from that base.

I had flown as first navigator throughout the course.

The next day was the 28th of January and a colleague and I were told that we would be leaving West Freugh the next day, as we had been posted to the Pathfinder Navigation Training Unit (PFNTU) at Warboys in Cambridgeshire. The reason for this was that we had shown exceptional ability in navigation. We were astonished. We had been given to understand that it was only operational crews who passed through Warboys to be trained in pathfinder techniques but that, of course, could have been *duff gen* (wrong information).

The following day we were to catch the night train from Stranraer to Euston. The train was packed and it was difficult to find a seat. We spotted what appeared to be two seats in a compartment but a naval officer barred the door and said there was no room. We said that we had a bottle of scotch. Oh, that was different, and he welcomed us in! The train started on time but it was to be the beginning of a dreadful journey which took almost 24 hours before we pulled into Euston. There was no food on the train and all we were able to do was to grab a bite to eat from the station buffet when we made one of the many stops on the way. It was the train on which a baby died from lack of milk, which became a front page story.

We eventually arrived at Warboys, a day late and rather weary.

◆ ◆ ◆

~ CHAPTER XIII ~

Pathfinder Navigation Training Unit, RAF Warboys, Cambridgeshire

R AF Warboys was quite out of the ordinary. It was a wartime airfield and had been one of the original bases when the Pathfinder Force was created. As the Force expanded it was necessary to have a base for training so the operational squadrons were moved elsewhere and Warboys became renowned for training the immediate future PFF crews. It was commanded at the time I was there by Group Captain "Dixie" Dean, a veteran bomber pilot who had been decorated with a DSO and a DFC and it was staffed by very experienced officers of all the disciplines from pilots to air gunners all of whom had a "gong". My colleague and I were objects of some interest but it soon became known why we were there.

At this stage in the war some Lancaster PFF Squadrons carried two navigators, Nav 1 to do the plotting with Nav 2 (sometimes known as Observer/Set operator or simply Set Operator) to work the radar. At Warboys we were trained in both roles, although the emphasis was on radar operation, as it was felt that we had already been well trained in plotting and radar operation was something that was completely new to us. We were taught how to operate Gee, H2S, Oboe and Loran, although as it would appear that we would be destined for a Lancaster Squadron it would be unlikely that we would have operational experience of Oboe and Loran.

The course was intensive and there was little time for leisure. However we did have one week-end off in the middle of the course and I arranged to meet Barbara in Peterborough. She travelled from Nottingham by train and I caught a local bus. We had an enjoyable day and I saw her safely on to the train in the evening. I went to the bus station and, to my surprise, found that there was no bus back to Warboys for the rest of that day, nor was there any bus that would go anywhere near it, so I decided I would have to walk. It turned out to be about twenty miles!

I flew fifteen times from Warboys in Lancasters, almost all by day and all at 17,000 feet, which meant my first experience of using oxygen. On the final flight the pilot was a Squadron Leader who assessed me and passed me for transfer to a squadron as a spare navigator versed in the two roles. The following day, 13th March, I was posted to number 35 Squadron at RAF Graveley in Huntingdonshire (now Cambridgeshire).

◆ ◆ ◆

Epilogue

Almost two years since I had reported to ACRC I had finally finished my training, but no doubt would have more to learn when I joined a squadron.

By and large I had enjoyed those two years, much of which was spent moving around and, to a lesser extent, hanging about.

I had many experiences, had seen other parts of the world and had the opportunity to view wonderful scenery and beautiful landscapes.

I had mixed with people from many walks of life, which had given me a wider understanding of humanity.

I had made many friends and had received very good instruction from the many "old hands" who had taught me.

I was now ready to put that which I had learned into practice on Number 35 Squadron, one of the original Pathfinder Squadrons, which I felt privileged to join.

◆ ◆ ◆

Part II
Operations in
War & Peace

N o. 35 was first formed on 1st February 1916 as a squadron of the Royal Flying Corps and went on to serve with distinction on the Western Front in support of a cavalry regiment. Reformed in 1929 as a bomber squadron, 35 continued in that role during the 1930s. After the outbreak of World War Two No.35 was initially involved in training, becoming part No.17 OTU on 8th April 1940.

On 5th November 1940, No.35 was reborn as an operational bomber squadron, the first in the RAF equipped with the new Handley Page Halifax aircraft, which carried out their first raid on 10th March 1941.

In August 1942 the squadron was on of five selected to form the new **Pathfinder Force** (No. 8 Group), remaining with that unit until the end of the war. In March 1944 the squadron converted to the Avro Lancaster.

LOCATION

25 August-7 December 1939: Cranfield
7 December 1939-1 February 1940: Bassingbourn
1 February-8 April 1940: Upwood
5-20 November 1940: Boscombe Downe
20 November-5 December 1940: Leeming
5 December 1940-15 August 1942: Linton-on-Ouse
15 August 1942-18 September 1946: Graveley, to join No. 8 (PFF) Group

AIRCRAFT

April 1938-February 1940: Fairey Battle
February 1939-April 1940: Avro Anson
November 1939-April 1940: Blenheim Mk IV
November 1940-February 1942: Handley Page Halifax B I
January 1942-March 1944: Handley Page Halifax B II
December 1943-March 1944: Handley Page Halifax B III
March 1944-October 1949: Avro Lancaster I and Avro Lancaster III

Squadron Code: TL
Squadron Motto: *Uno animo agimus* (We act with one accord)

GROUP AND DUTY

On 26 September 1939: Pool squadron with No.6 Group
8 April 1940: Merges with No.207 Squadron to become No.17 OTU
From November 1940-August 1942: Bomber squadron with No.4 Group
From August 1942: Pathfinder squadron with No.8 (PFF) Group

Preface to Part Two

I concluded Part I on on 13th March 1945, the date I was posted from Pathfinder Navigation Training Unit (PFNTU) RAF Warboys to 35 Squadron at RAF Graveley. It was not originally my intention to recount what happened after that but I was told that my initial account was not long enough for publication, so I decided to write about what happened in the following two years with the hope that the extended work might be suitable (and this, happily, has proved to be the case).

In Part One I avoided naming people, just detailing the work for which they were responsible but in the following account I have decided to use names, which makes the narrative more interesting.

I will again mention that I kept no diaries (not allowed at the time) but I have, however, the benefit of my RAF log book and a scrapbook which covers a small part of those two years. Apart from those, I again have to rely on memory, which may be clouded by time, although I believe my account to be substantially accurate.

◆ ◆ ◆

Bowen-Morris and crew, April 1945.

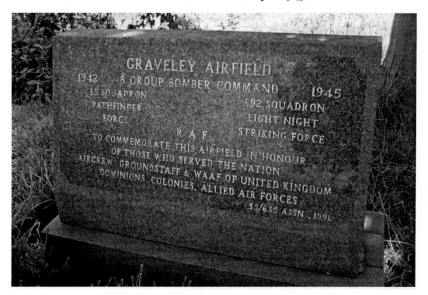

*The plaque erected in 1991 at the entrance
to the farm on which RAF Graveley was built.*

~ CHAPTER XIV ~

RAF Graveley, Huntingdonshire, a Pathfinder Force (PFF) Base

R AF Graveley was a wartime airfield, one of many in East Anglia. The airfield and the operating and administrative buildings were on the left of an unclassified road which ran north west to Offord D'Arcy, with the Messes and accommodation huts on the right side of that road. The airfield was a typical Bomber Command Base with a perimeter of five miles or thereabouts. There was one long tarmac runway, along which FIDO[1] pipes had been installed. Those pipes stood proud of the ground by about nine inches. They proved their worth when planes returning from Ops were confronted by fog over base. Not many airfields were thus equipped, so on occasions Graveley had a number of visitors. It was, in fact, the first airfield to be so equipped, probably because it was a Pathfinder base.

The airfield had been built on farmland as would have been the case with nearly all the wartime airfields, and was

---

[1] Fog obscuring their home airfields was such a hazard to RAF aircraft returning from bombing operations that in 1942 Winston Churchill, ordered the Petroleum Warfare Department to develop a way of dispersing it. The result was FIDO (Fog, Intensive, Dispersal Of) a network of pipes and petrol burners capable of clearing fog from runways. It was installed at 15 airfields around the UK. Burning petrol at the rate of 100,000 gallons per hour, FIDO produced sufficient heat to lift fog and enable pilots to land safely when visibility would otherwise have been zero. Between 1943 and 1945 2,500 aircraft landed safely in fog thanks to FIDO, saving the lives of many aircrew. FIDO also helped shorten the war by allowing operations to continue in poor weather when flying would otherwise have been impossible.

still being used for that purpose on the parts that were not required for operational use.

There was one other Pathfinder squadron based at Graveley. It was 692, one of the nine squadrons of the Light Night Striking Force (LNSF)

The accommodation huts and the messes were all built on the Nissen principle. The former, from memory, had ten beds on either side of the hut with a coke burning stove in the centre. The beds were comfortable and there was no shortage of blankets Again, from memory, there was limited furniture for clothes.

The toilets, washing and showering facilities were on the same site but the latter could not always be relied on to produce hot water!

There was ample parking space on that site for cars and motor bikes for those fortunate to have them.

The Officers' Mess was comfortable. It had two main areas; a comfortable lounge and a dining hall. The lounge was furnished with carpet and comfortable arm chairs. There was a good supply of newspapers and magazines. The dining hall was spacious and had good quality tables and chairs. The crockery and cutlery was of a good standard and the food was acceptable. We were waited upon by WAAF who were always pleasant, possibly hand picked to keep the spirits up. There was a vestibule where the Squadron's trophies and silverware was displayed and, of course, there was a Bar – absolutely essential!

The Sergeants' Mess was of a similar standard but I had no occasion to go there.

◆ ◆ ◆

~ CHAPTER XV ~

The Last Days of War
13th March to 8th May 1945

No 35 Squadron was one of the founder members of The Pathfinder Force (PFF) which came into being in August 1942 as 8 Group, commanded by Air Vice Marshal Donald Bennett. On the date that I joined the Squadron it was commanded by Wing Commander (later Group Captain) H.J.E. "Speedy" Le Good DSO, DFC.

On 13 March 1945 I set foot on RAF Graveley which had been a short ride in RAF transport from PFNTU Warboys.

I reported to the Adjutant of the Squadron, who called an airman to show me the hut where I would be sleeping and to take my luggage. That was the extent of my welcome, not that I had expected anything more. I was then left to my own devices. I went to the Mess for dinner but I cannot recall having been spoken to by anyone.

It must be realised that there was a great deal of tension on a Bomber base. There were crews who had been waiting that day to learn whether they would be operating that night, one further trip to count towards their tour of thirty. I cannot remember whether there were ops that night but, if there were, they all returned safely. However, they must have been mindful of the fact that a few days earlier the Squadron had lost one of its most experienced pilots, S/Ldr Danny Everett DSO,DFC** who had been on his ninety-ninth op! He had been shot down over Hamburg and was killed along with the whole of his experienced crew.

The tension was not confined to the aircrew. The ground crews, who worked so hard to service the aircraft and to repair damage resulting from enemy flak and fighters, which was often quite extensive, had deadlines to meet and were not immune from stress. There was also a constant change of personnel. Crews who had finished their tour of thirty ops were posted away, quite often on the following day, or they would be more likely going on leave to be notified during that time where their next posting would be. Sadly, of course, there were crews that would not return from an operational flight. They would have been shot down by fighters or flak, killed, injured or taken prisoner. It was also possible that an aircraft would be so damaged that, in spite of the efforts of the crew, it would crash on the way home or on an attempted landing. Crews tended to stick together in their off-duty hours and would often go to one of the local pubs.

Taking into account all of the above factors, it was not surprising that no one was interested in me. I had come to Graveley as a spare navigator, versed in both the roles of plotter and observer/set operator (Radar-Gee and H2S). The squadron's Lancasters at that time often carried two navigators and thus there was a crew of eight. It was some time later that it became clear that the bomb aimers were to be trained to work the radar as a blind bombing technique, developed using H2S.

It was not often that a spare navigator was needed. One had to wait until that particular crew member reported sick or there was some other rare reason why he was unable to fly. I had to be patient.

Bored stiff after more than a week with nothing constructive to do, I decided to go to the Squadron Adjutant and offer my services to lend him a hand. He was so pleased to accept and gave me a few things to do to see how I coped. He was under stress with the work and responsibility entailed in the administration of a squadron. A former World War One officer, he had been recalled to the Service.

My suggestion worked well and it was not long before I became known as the ex officio Assistant Adjutant. Because I was nearly always in the office adjacent to the Adjutant, I came to the notice of many personnel and at last it was realised that I had joined the Squadron.

As a result of this I was informed on 26th March that I would be flying twice that day, in the morning with F/O Henderson and after lunch with S/Ldr Gooch, the O/C "B" Flight. They were to be short training flights: the first, bombing and the second, fighter affiliation (F/A). I was obs/set op and the duration of both flights was just over two hours. Nothing was said to me afterwards, so I presumed that my work had been satisfactory.

On 9th April the role for which I had trained over the previous two years came to fruition. I was informed that the obs/set op in F/Lt Bob Newbiggin's crew had reported sick and I would be taking his place. There was I, untried and untested on operations, filling a gap in a very experienced crew. Bob was an Australian, a big man, a surfing champion. I shall never forget the kindness and understanding of that crew, in particular the skipper. They made me welcome. I attended briefing. We were going to Kiel as visual centrers. We were told that there were enemy ships in the Canal, which were expected to try to make a break for it and go to Sweden, and the purpose of the raid was to prevent that happening. We were to take off at 2000 hours.

After the standard pre-op meal of egg and bacon and collection of parachutes we were ferried out to Lancaster "TL E" (TL was the identification code for 35 Squadron and E the aircraft letter). What I particularly liked about Bob and his crew was that they did not fuss. They would have been aware that I was well trained and knew my way around the inside of a Lancaster, and they were happy for me to prove myself.

We clambered aboard. I took up my position at the table to the left of Nav 1 (the plotter) facing the left side of the fuselage behind the pilot. I had the H2S set in front of my head with the screen angled to suit my vision and the Gee set to my left. The skipper and the flight engineer did the pre flight check and the former then called each crew member in turn to check that they and their equipment were fit and ready to go.

We waited our turn to be called forward from our dispersal point and suddenly there was a startling experience. A Mosquito of 692 Squadron was being "bombed up" on the other side of the airfield when something went wrong and there was an explosion. The sound was so severe that it penetrated the fuselage of our Lanc and we also heard the noise over our headphones.

It shook our crew but we had a job to do and we had to get on with it.

We soon had the signal to roll forward to the runway and were then given the green light to take off. I pulled across the curtain at the back of the two navigators to shut out any light that may have interfered with our work. I was conscious of the Lanc levelling out when we reached our operating height and the turns from time to time, but apart from that

I was so busy getting fixes on Gee and passing them to Nav 1 that I had little time for anything else. Time went quickly and it seemed that we were soon over our aiming point and dropped our flares.

It was then that Bob said to me, "You can come out from behind that curtain now Peter and see what's going on."

Looking out of a window on the starboard side I saw seemingly innocuous puffs of coloured smoke that were in reality deadly balls of tracer from anti-aircraft guns. It was at that point that we were coned by searchlights and subjected to intense anti-aircraft fire. By quick reaction and skilful airmanship Bob brought the Lanc out of that predicament and we set course for home.

We landed safely back at Graveley after a flight of five hours and five minutes. So ended my first op. I had been apprehensive but not afraid. I was pleased with my performance, which I felt had been efficient. After de-briefing I had a drink of something and then was glad to go to bed. The following morning I learnt that our Lanc had flak damage in several places.

I was told that I would remain with Bob and his crew until his obs/set op was fit again to fly.

On the following day I flew again with Bob and his crew. This time it was a daylight op as visual centrers with the target at Bayreuth. We would be a part of a small specialist force. I cannot remember the purpose of that operation but it certainly wasn't to attend the Festival! We took off at 1200 hours and had an uneventful trip to the target with me again using Gee and passing the fixes to Nav 1. We dropped our flares on target and then headed for home. We had not experienced any anti-aircraft activity.

After a short while Bob came through to me on the inter com and said, "I know you started to train as a pilot. Would you like to have a go at flying this beast?"

I jumped at the opportunity. There was not much room in the cockpit of a Lanc but he managed to vacate his seat and help me in. I really enjoyed sitting in that seat but have to admit that there was not a lot for me to do but to keep an eye on the instruments and ask Bob what action I should take if anything needed to be done. I was so happy to have had that opportunity that it did not occur to me until a long while later that we did not know whether or not there were still enemy fighters about. I am sure that neither did Bob have that thought because if we were to have been attacked I would not have had much of a clue what to do. Perhaps he had been assured at the briefing that there should not be any fighters in that area.

We landed back at Graveley after a trip five minutes short of six hours.

I flew twice more with Bob. These were two short training flights similar to those the previous month, F/A and S.B.A (Standard Beam Approach). I was sorry to have to leave that crew.

On 18 April I was asleep in bed in the hut when I felt someone shaking me. It was the batman.

"Wake up Sir, you are flying with the Master Bomber."

I asked him to repeat what he had said because I could not believe my ears.

"Yes Sir, you are flying with the Master Bomber."

I still doubted what I had heard but I quickly washed and shaved and had a rushed breakfast before hurrying to the briefing room, where I learnt that we were to take off at 1100 hours. Our C/O, Wing Cdr "Speedy" Le Good, was the Master

Bomber and his crew was made up of the leaders of the sections for Navigation, Bomb Aiming, Wireless Operation, Flight Engineer and the deputy Gunnery Leader. A crew of men at the very top of their respective roles with one exception – me, as obs/set op.

There were four Squadron Leaders, two Flight Lieutenants and one humble Flying Officer (me). I had no idea why I had been chosen to fly with such a distinguished crew but it was likely that it was just because I was spare and had proved myself with Bob.

I was to undertake my normal role and in addition to take down as best I could the Master Bomber's instructions over the target to the other Pathfinder aircraft and the Main Force. It was to be a major operation with almost one thousand aircraft. The target was Heligoland, a fortified island naval base with an airfield, and the brief was to completely destroy the island.

The Lancaster on this important trip was "S" for Sugar. It was no different from the other aircraft on the Squadron and was, in fact, the very one in which I had flown on those training flights a few days earlier.

I took up my position at the table with Squadron Leader Harry Wright DFC* as Nav 1 on my right. We took off on time and as far as I was aware we reached the target without any problems. I took hold of a pad ready to record the MB's instructions. That was a fascinating experience. Unfortunately, because I was engrossed in my task I was unable to have a look out of a window to see what was going on but I had a running commentary. I have no idea for how long we were over the target but it must have been lengthy, having regard to our role. We eventually set course for home and safely landed at Graveley after a flight of four hours, thirty minutes. I was again pleased with my performance. I attended debriefing and was told that Speedy was pleased with my record of his instructions.

On 1st May I was crewed as obs/set op with F/O Bowen-Morris as skipper. This was a permanent position (unless something happened to end it). It was not until some years later that I found out that Bowen-Morris, in Lancaster "K" had been attacked by a night fighter on 14th April over Belgium. The aircraft had been set on fire. The whole crew baled out. One was killed but the others survived, although the skipper and one other were injured.

The following day, 2 May, I flew with Bowen-Morris for the first time. It was a short training flight cross country and SBA.

On 7 May we were briefed to take part in *Operation Manna*, the dropping of food to the starving Dutch. From memory we marked the aiming point at Tegelberg, a field near Rotterdam. A humanitarian trip; so different from what the squadron had been doing since 1939. A truce had been agreed with the enemy to enable Bomber Command to help to alleviate the Dutch from their predicament. Nevertheless, we carried our gunners, just in case the message had not been heard!

The following day, the 8th of May 1945, the war in Europe ended.

◆ ◆ ◆

~ CHAPTER XVI ~

Victory and Afterwards
9th May to 31st December 1945

I cannot remember what I did on VE (Victory in Europe) Day. The squadron was, of course, still operational and some aircraft were dispatched to Lubek to bring back prisoners of war. My only memory of that day is having a quiet drink in the mess in the evening, thankful that the war in Europe was over but there were, of course, the Japanese still to be reckoned with.

We wondered what would be the future of the Squadron. It was not long before rumours began to circulate that Bomber Command was to be a part of *Tiger Force*, to be dispatched to the Far East to assist the war against that enemy. What I was not aware of, and it did not come to my notice until that war was over, was that 35 Squadron had, in fact, been selected for Tiger Force and would have been based in Okinawa. The squadron was to be re-equipped with new Lancasters, Mark B1FE, modified for service in the topics. This detailed information had been kept under wraps and I doubt that even our CO had been privy to it.

However, rumours notwithstanding, peacetime operations, so far as we were concerned, had to proceed. On May 10th we were detailed to fly to Lubek on *Operation Exodus*, to play our part in bringing home service personnel who two days previous to this had been prisoners of war. We were to carry twenty four. They were to be told that we would make them as comfortable as we could for a three-hour flight back to the UK. It was also to be explained to them that once seated they were on no account to move around, for fear of upsetting the aircraft trim. We stayed at the airfield overnight and we were obviously fed and presumably accommodated but my memory is blank as far as those functions were concerned. It was all rather weird because, only a few days previous to this, Lubek had been an active Luftwaffe base.

The following morning we loaded our passengers. Most of them were somewhat bemused, which was quite understandable. I did not have the opportunity to converse with any of them because the crew at the front of the Lanc had to board first, but apparently some of those waiting to be taken home had been incarcerated in POW camps since 1939 and some were apprehensive because they had never previously flown.

We landed safely back at Graveley and handed our charges over to an officer who would see them on to transport to a transit camp. It was imperative that they were to be well looked after and I have no doubt that they were. The outward flight was of three hours and fifteen minutes duration and the return three hours thirty minutes.

On May 17th we flew for one hour thirty minutes, shown in my log book simply as "Formation" with me as observer rather than obs/set op. There must have been some significance for this but I have no idea what.

On June 4th we flew a short cross country training flight lasting one hour forty minutes.

The war in Europe had been over for nearly one month. The Air Ministry had decided that, as a gesture to the ground crews who had worked so hard over a long period, they would be invited to fly on what were to be officially known as 'Cooks

Tours' – flights over Germany to see the extent of the damage inflicted by Bomber Command. On June 5th we took five ground crew on a trip lasting almost six hours. We flew over Wesel, Ruhr, Hanover, Bremen and Munster. We indulged in quite a lot of low flying. I found the trip quite awesome and could not help but spare a thought for the civilian men, women and children who had suffered in Bomber Command's air raids; a sad consequence of war.

An Aussie pilot who was going home had a motorbike to sell; a 1937 600cc Panther with twin exhausts, in good condition. Having had motorbike experience I bought it for £55. It would be useful for journeys to home and to Barbara's home at West Bridgford, near Nottingham.

At about that time our flight engineer, who was a car buff and owned an Austin Seven in fine condition, told us that there was a 1925 bull-nosed Morris for sale for £25, which he thought would make an ideal means of transport to get to the pub in the evenings. Most of the crews apparently went to those in the area of St Neot's, where there was quite a choice. We clubbed together and bought the car. It was in pretty good condition but the hood would need some attention before long. One thing that fascinated me was the headlamp dipper, which was controlled by a lever about the length of the handbrake. It was really only a five seater but all seven of us managed to cram in. This was only on rare occasions as on most evenings not all of us wanted to drink and preferred a quiet evening in the Mess.

On June 19th we flew a cross-country training flight of just over two hours and on the following day I flew as navigator on a 20-minute flight to RAF Upwood and, according to my log book, flew back to Graveley shortly afterwards with P/O Mercer as pilot and me as passenger in a different Lanc.

On the following day I flew as navigator to RAF Wyton on a flight of twenty minutes but for some reason there is no entry in my log book as to how I got back to Graveley. It must have been by RAF transport.

On 26th June I flew as Instructor, with W/O Smith as pilot on a short cross-country.

On 29th June there was again a short trip of twenty minutes to RAF Upwood and presumably RAF transport, as before, for the return to Graveley.

On 6th July another formation flight but the aircraft was found to be unserviceable (U/S) after a few minutes and we returned to base.

On 9th July we flew a second Cooks Tour, this time over The Hague, Dortmund, Cologne and Aachen. Three hours forty five minutes.

On 25th July came something completely different. I was bomb aimer on a two-hour trip to Cardigan Bay, to drop unarmed bombs into the bay with the flight described as 'bomb disposal'.

On 28th July, shortly after breakfast, the Tannoy announced "Flying Officer Bowen-Morris and crew to report immediately to the Briefing Room". Waiting there was the CO, who told us that the War Office and the Air Ministry had for some time been exploring the feasibility of bringing home some of the Eighth Army from Italy in the Command's Lancasters. It had been found to be possible and it was now necessary to do a proving flight. The Ministry had opted for 35 Squadron and he had chosen our crew. We would not be taking our gunners and Nav 1 would stand down to be replaced by the Nav Leader, S/Ldr Harry Wright DFC*. We were to take off at 1100 hours and fly to RAF Elsham Wolds to pick up freight. This was the equipment needed to control aircraft landing and taking off from the base in Italy. We would be accommodated at Elsham Wolds overnight and would take off at 0900 hours the next morning to fly to Pomigliano, the airport for Naples. We would have to go 'the long way round', as we would not be permitted to fly over the countries which had been neutral.

We duly arrived at RAF Elsham Wolds in north Lincolnshire after a forty-minute flight. We supervised the loading of the freight into the bomb bay and ensured that it was safely and securely stowed. I spent the remainder of that day in the Mess and had an early night. We took off at 0920 hours and set course for Land's End. I carried out my usual job of obtaining fixes on Gee and handing them to Nav 1. Upon reaching the point where we would leave the UK behind, Nav 1 gave our skipper the course for Coruna on the northwest coast of Spain. This would be the point where we would lose the service of Gee, or so I had calculated. We flew over the Bay of Biscay and located the point at which we would need a slight change of course to follow the Spanish and then the Portuguese coasts on our port side, until we reached the Straits of Gibraltar.

It was a glorious summer's day and I am sure that Nav 1 and I had no problems with navigation. On this leg we kept the coasts in sight but had to be careful not to encroach on 'neutral' air space. This part of the flight gave me an opportunity to test my skills with H2S.

In due time we turned to port and flew over the Straits. Nav 1 then gave a course to our skipper which would take us over the Mediterranean to a point in southern Italy which, when we turned north, would enable us to fly over Vesuvius (we were not going to miss that opportunity!) on our way to

Pomigliano, where we landed safely after a flight of exactly seven hours.

We supervised the unloading of our freight and were debriefed. We would be taking twenty passengers back to the UK. They were at a transit camp somewhere in the area and would be taken to Pomigliano sometime the next day. We would take off early on the day after that, so we had a day to spare when we would be left to our own devices.

I decided to have a walk around Naples and most probably hitched a ride in one of the many army vehicles that were around. There is a saying "see Naples and die" although it was more appropriate at that time to smell Naples and die! I presumed that the sewage system had been damaged during the war and had not been repaired.

Naples is, of course, an ancient city having been the capital of the kingdom of Naples from the year 1138. It has passed through the hands of the French, Spanish and Austrians in the course of its chequered existence, where the first two mentioned had control more than once as it changed hands on a number of occasions.

I found it to be a fascinating place with many types of architecture and some very attractive buildings. It has fine churches and museums which contain many works of art. It did not appear to have been damaged to any extent during the course of the war (although that may not have been the case in the parts that I did not have time to visit).

I came across an interesting jewellers shop and decided to see if I could find something attractive to take back to my girlfriend Barbara. I came across a ring with matching earrings delicately fashioned in silver filigree. I cannot remember how much it cost but it did not appear expensive and I thought it would appeal to her.

The following morning we loaded our passengers and made them as comfortable as we could for their seven-hour flight to the UK but stressed that they must not leave their seats without permission for fear of upsetting the aircraft trim. We hoped that they had been advised to empty their bladders before boarding!

We took off at 0930 hours bound for RAF Glatton, near Peterborough. We flew the reverse of the track that we had followed on the outward journey. The weather was again glorious and we landed at our destination after an uneventful trip lasting just short of seven hours. As we disembarked our passengers I had the thought of having participated, once again, in an operation which had a humanitarian theme.

We took off at 1650 hours for a ten minute flight back to Graveley.

In between the flights of the previous three months I had continued my work as Assistant Adjutant and had spent some time studying for an examination.

I see that in my log book for that trip my role was shown as 2nd navigator. Why this was I have no memory but it may have been that a navigator (or perhaps a number of them) had protested at having to describe himself as an obs/set op when he wore a navigator's badge which had been well earned.

We had been debriefed when we returned and as a result of our successful trip the Air Ministry decided to proceed with the operation of bringing back some of the Eighth Army in Bomber Command's Lancs. It would be known as Operation Dodge and would proceed forthwith.

Soon after that decision was taken it was decided to expand the operation and establish a base at Bari on the Adriatic coast, on almost the same latitude as Naples.

On 16th August came a second trip on Operation Dodge, this time to Bari. We took off at 0700 hours and followed a similar course to that on the previous occasion, when we left Land's End. The only other change was when we reached southern Italy we set course for Bari. Another uneventful trip, again of seven hours.

We were there for three more days. It appeared to be a poverty stricken area around the airfield but I did not venture into the town.

On 20th August we took off at 0630 again with twenty soldiers. This time our destination was RAF Tibbenham in Norfolk. The trip was uneventful and we landed after a flight of seven hours thirty five minutes.

We took off at 15.30 for the short flight back to base but an engine failed and after ten minutes we landed back at Tibbenham on three engines. We had to ditch Lancaster 'E' and I flew back to base with F/O Brown in one of the other Lancs.

On 13th September we were selected to fly to Brussels on Operation 'Liberty'. My memory fails me and I cannot remember what the purpose was. For some reason we had to fly first to RAF Wyton to pick up someone or something. However, it must have been someone because we had to return them to Wyton afterwards, having stayed in Brussels overnight. The flights were 1½ hours each way.

On 19th September came Operation Dodge number №51. This gives some indication of the many hundreds of the Eighth Army that had been brought back to Britain in the Command's Lancs. It also implies that here had been an operation every day since our proving flight as that was the number of days that had elapsed.

It was to be a memorable flight.

We took off from Graveley at 0700 hours and landed at Bari after a flight of seven hours once again. We were told that we would be there for one day and fly back on the 21st. The ground staff at Bari, in their spare time, had fashioned small motor boats from drop tanks and aircraft starter motors. I think this must have had official blessing as they would have been only too obvious to anyone looking around. I decided to sample what these small craft were like and found three airmen to accompany me. We launched the little tub and made our way in to the Adriatic. About a mile from the shore the engine conked out and despite our efforts, pulling on the handle, we could not persuade it to restart. As the senior person of the four, I said that we would have to abandon the boat and swim back. The response from all three was "We cannot swim!"

"Aircrew that cannot swim?" I thought. But maybe they were, in fact, ground staff. There was nothing for it but for me to swim back alone and have them rescued. I had just about reached the point where I found *terra firma* when I heard chugging. The others had managed to restart the engine!

Later that day there was a tragic accident. At any one time at Bari, and at Pomigliano, there were a large number of Lancs on the airfield. They were parked parallel to the runway but a fair distance from it and were angled so that it was possible to leave the rank without having to move any of the others so parked. A Lancaster had a tendency, on occasions, to swing to the left on take-off. This happened to one that afternoon and sadly the pilot was unable to correct the swing and his Lanc ploughed into those that were parked. We left Bari shortly after this and never found out how many had been killed or injured or how many Lancs had been written off.

We were understandably shaken by what had happened but we delivered twenty more soldiers safely to Tibbenham.

Shortly afterwards, we took off for base, and to our horror we experienced a swing on take-off. Tibbenham was equipped with FIDO, so over the pipe we went. Bowen Morris over corrected the swing so over the pipe we went on the starboard side. He skilfully corrected that swing and we were back on the runway. However, as the reader may appreciate, we were now well down the runway. We were too far to abort the take off and had to trust to luck and our skipper that we still had sufficient runway to take off. Thanks to Bowen-Morris's skilful airmanship we just made it! That incident illustrates how much trust members of a crew had in each other. An eventful day!

On 5th and 8th October I had two short flights as navigator to F/Lt Heavery AFC, DFM on GCA (Ground Controlled Approach) exercises.

Sometime in November came another big change. All wartime service personnel, apart from the regulars, were given a demob number. This was so that demobilisation was properly controlled and spread over a long period. It was possible to override that number if there were extenuating circumstances to justify an earlier release. It will be appreciated that these systems caused crews to break up. It was one of my jobs as Assistant Adjutant to assist in ensuring that at any one time we always had as many complete crews as was possible. This, of course, meant that there were frequent movements within crews.

Because of these problems and the decision of the Government to gradually reduce the number of squadrons in the RAF, 156 Squadron (a Pathfinder Squadron based at Upwood) was disbanded and many of that Squadron's personnel transferred to 35 Squadron. One result of this was that I was transferred to a crew from 156, which was short of a 2nd navigator. A very experienced crew skippered by F/O Gill Hampson DFC, whose wireless operator was F/O Pete Skingsley DFC and whose other four members, nav 1, flight engineer and the two gunners were warrant officers. I was the least experienced once again.

Gill, I was to find out later, was a skilful pilot. He was a very modest, reserved character who was very much a loner and took some getting to know but he and I were very compatible.

Pete Skingsley was one of life's characters. He was at Kings School, Canterbury when, at seventeen years old, he ran away from school, put his age up to eighteen (in my experience we were never asked for proof of age) and volunteered for aircrew. He was impatient and could not face the long period training to be a pilot, so was accepted for training as a wireless op. He had completed a tour of ops and been awarded the DFC before he was eighteen! He and I, together with Robin Butterell, also a navigator, would often be found in one another's company a little later on. Robin had been born on the same day as me!

On 7th November I had my first flight with Gill. It was a further Operation Dodge, this time to Pomigliano. However, we had to fly first to RAF Glatton to pick up twenty passengers for the outward journey. I am pretty sure it was not the wish of former Eighth Army soldiers to return! It may have been RAF personnel making the trip to replace those at Pomigliano who were due for leave.

We had left Graveley at 0615 hours, in the dark, and took off for our destination at 0820. It was an uneventful trip lasting six hours and twenty minutes. We were there for a day and were to make the return flight to Glatton on the ninth. This time we were to have twenty members of the Pioneer Corps as our passengers, a sergeant and 19 privates. It would appear that none of them had previously flown, so we did our best to keep them calm.

We took off at 0730 hours and landed safely at Glatton after seven hours twenty minutes. This time, for some reason, I was first off the Lanc, through the front exit. I think Gill may have asked me to see that our soldiers were all right. As I walked towards them the sergeant came up to me, smartly saluted and said,

"Sir, we would like you to have this with our grateful thanks for bringing us home; we have all been away since 1939!" He produced a wad of currency notes.

"Thank you sergeant for that kind gesture," I responded, "but we could not possibly accept your gift. We were doing our job and are glad that we were able to bring you back to the UK. I wish you well for the future."

This was to be the final Operation Dodge for our crew. I understand that the Operation was brought to an end shortly after this. Some hundreds, possibly thousands, of soldiers of the Eighth Army had been brought back to the UK by the Command's Lancasters. When one thinks about it, the cost must have been considerable. I do not have the means to compare that with the cost that there would have been had they all been returned by ship .That would have been an interesting comparison but the exercise would not be feasible. It was a great humanitarian operation and I am glad that I had been able to participate.

The 13th November was my first night flight with Gill. We took off at 1730 hours on a cross country training exercise described as a 'night cross country' with a route from base – Lincoln – Blackpool – Stoke – Shrewsbury – Northampton – base. It lasted two hours ten minutes. I am shown in my log book as Nav II (Roman numerals!) so it would seem that the title of my role had changed once again.

On 19th November we had a twenty-five minute flight to RAF Tibbenham and flew back to base in the same aircraft four days later. I cannot remember what the purpose was but it may have been to repair something on the Lanc that could not be carried out at base.

I did not fly at all in December, so carried on with my duties to assist the Adjutant and continued with my studies. I was fortunate to be granted leave to spend my twenty first birthday at home with my parents, my fiancée Barbara (we had become engaged the previous August) and my younger brother Alan and his girlfriend, who later became his wife.

◆ ◆ ◆

~ CHAPTER XVII ~

Operation 'Sinkum'
1st January to 31st March 1946

On New Year's Day we flew a night cross country, taking off at 1900 hours (possibly to ensure that any hangovers were out of the way). We were in the air for two hours forty minutes. I see from my Log Book that this was the first occasion that we were required to show which mark of Lanc we were using. On this flight it was Mark II.

On January 10th for some reason I was passenger in a Lanc Mark VII piloted by F/O Cornelius on a thirty minute trip to RAF Woodbridge. As a matter of interest Woodbridge had been a major diversionary airfield for aircraft in trouble whilst on, or returning from, ops during the war. On the return to base I am recorded as 'Nav II' with Gill as pilot in a Lanc, again a Mark VII.

My Log Book for January was signed off by S/Ldr M. Beetham DFC, O.C. A Flt. You will read more of Mike Beetham later.

Some days later that month all the Squadron's aircrew and ground crew were called to the briefing room. The Squadron Commander said that he had received a Movement Order from the Air Ministry, transferring the Squadron to an airfield in Egypt, one of the bases established between the wars. During the next few days our Lancasters would be exchanged for brand new Lancs Mark FE1, the Mark that we would have had earlier had we been based in Okinawa. There would have to be some changes in personnel as there would be no point in taking those whose demob numbers may be imminent. Officers would receive their tropical kit allowance and the NCOs and airmen would be issued with the bog standard tropical kit. He was unable to tell us at that time when we would leave Graveley for good but he hoped that he would be in a position to grant leave before we left.

For some of us it was an exciting prospect; for those who were married or engaged, probably not so.

I phoned Barbara to tell her. She was pleased for me but not really happy at the news. I asked her father if he would give his blessing to our being married before I went. The answer was an emphatic "no". We were disappointed but, on reflection, I think he was right at the time.

I went to Gieves and Hawkes in London to be fitted for my kit; jacket, trousers, shirts, shorts, socks and underwear. The black shoes to be worn were no different from those we wore in the UK. I would leave the purchase of sandals until we were there. Worn with the normal forage cap or peaked cap the tropical kit was very smart.

Pending more news of the move to Egypt, the squadron continued with training and taking part in the various jobs that were found for us.

On 9th February was a cross-country training flight lasting two hours forty five minutes in Lanc 'E' mark VII.

On 18th February an Air Test in Lanc 'E', lasting just over one hour.

On 21st February came a first flight in a brand new Lanc mark FE1, so it would appear that the posting to Egypt was not far ahead. The description in my log book is 'NFT' – which I presume were the initials for New Flight Test. It could not have been Night Flying Test as it was carried out in daylight.

On 27th February it was bomb disposal, which now had an operational name – 'Sinkum'! We flew first to RAF Tuddenham, to load the bombs. Two hours later we took off at 1400 hours to sink the bombs in Cardigan Bay and return to base after two hours forty five minutes. The final twenty five minutes of that flight are shown in my log book in red ink, which indicates that it was then night. Authority was very strict in matters like this.

On 28th February I was taken as a passenger in Lanc 'P', skippered by F/Lt Clarine DFC, on a twenty minute flight to Tuddenham and returned to base six hours later in Lanc 'C' skippered by Gill. I have no idea what that was all about and rather strangely my log book does not show the mark of those two Lancs.

On 14th March was Operation 'Sinkum' again; a flight lasting two hours and five minutes in Lanc 'E' mark FE1.

On 18th March my log book reads (with pilot Gill and me as Nav II) "X/C A/C U/S D.N.C.O." which translates as Cross Country, Aircraft Unserviceable, Duty not carried out. It also strangely shows the manufacturer's number SW313 and the Squadron letter 'B'. That was the first, and would be the only time I was required to show the manufacturer's number.

On 28th March another Sinkum to Cardigan Bay, but this time combined with a cross country exercise, flying in formation. We wondered what the formation presaged.

It must have been around this time, or it could have been earlier, that all the Squadron personnel were again called to the Briefing Room. There, our CO told us that the UK government had received a message from their Egyptian counterparts which read that King Farouk did not want us to establish a base in his country and we would not be welcome. So ended that possibility. The CO went on to say that he had no doubt that the Air Ministry would soon find something else for us to do.

The 35 Squadron crest.

~ CHAPTER XVIII ~

Showpiece Squadron
1st April to 7th July 1946

E arly in April we were once again assembled in the Briefing Room where our new CO, W/Cdr Alan Craig DSO, DFC, said that he had some good news.

"The Air Ministry has decided that 35 Squadron will be the Showpiece Squadron of the RAF, the Flagship. We will be giving formation flight displays both nationally and internationally. This is a prestigious appointment for our famous Squadron.

The formation will be made of four triangles, each of three aircraft. I will be the leader with my two flight commanders, with S/Ldr Mike Beetham DFC to port and S/Ldr "Shorty" Harris DFC to starboard, on my flanks, slightly to the rear. The fourth three will bring up the rear. We will wait to see whether those three might be better positioned in line.

The flight commanders will chose the twelve pilots for the formation. The remaining four aircraft of the Squadron will act as spares. However, on all practise flights one of them will take the place of one of the chosen twelve, which will stand down. One of the chosen twelve will take my place as leader for that practise.

All formation navigators and wireless operators will carry out their normal duties on every formation operation, whether it be training or display. This is essential so that if one of the aircraft should have a problem which necessitates a return to base or diversion to an emergency base, the skipper will know where he is.

Practise is essential. A Lancaster has not been designed to fly in close formation and the pilots will have to exercise great skill to keep in formation. Depending on the weather, we will practise every day from now on until we achieve perfection. We will start tomorrow. Aircraft will take off in the sequence of their position in the formation and land likewise. A photographer from the Daily Sketch will be with us on some of the training flights, flying in a Cessna.

Best of luck, go to it!"

On 8th April was our first formation practise flight in Lanc mark FE1 "B". We were instructed to take position 5. It was a short trip of one hour fifty minutes to see how things worked out. Apparently no problems; we all landed safely and attended de-briefing.

On 9th April was our second formation practise in Lanc mark FE1 "E". The replacement of the whole of the Squadrons Lancs with mark FE1s was now complete. We were assigned "E" in which we were to fly on every occasion from then on unless the aircraft was unserviceable. We were also allocated position 6 on a permanent basis. The practise lasted the same amount of time as the previous one.

On 10th April came a further change in my role. We were briefed for a night cross country training flight concentrating on star shots with the astrograph. We were also to carry eight bombs for a practise drop. My log book shows that A/B (Air Bomber) was added to my role of Nav II. As I would be taking the astro shots as well, I was going to have a busy trip.

We wondered why there was emphasis on a night flight taking astro shots. This would seem to suggest that sometime in the immediate future we might be taking a long night flight with astro to back up whatever other navigation aids that we would have on that flight. This practise lasted five hours thirty five minutes in Lanc "G".

On 11th April a further formation practise, this time in number 2 position. Two hours duration.

On 12th April it was our turn as Leader in a practise flight of two hours. I think it must have been Alan Craig's idea for the pilots to change positions on each training flight. This gave them the opportunity of experiencing and perfecting the skills required of them in those different situations.

On 15th April more formation practise, this time in number 2 position in a flight of two hours.

Later that day, further practice bombing with me as A/B for two hours. These practise flights with Nav II as A/B would seem to indicate that the role of A/B would cease with Nav II training to bomb by H2S, and a different name being given to that combined role.

On 30th April two hours practise formation in number 6 position.

On 1st May forty minutes F/A in Lanc "D" with both Gill and F/Lt Clarine DFC as pilots.

On 2nd May a final two hour practise in number 6 position before our first international formation display, which was to be two days later.

The 4th of May was Dutch Liberation Day. One year had elapsed since they had been freed from the yoke of the Nazis. We took off at 11.30 hours and flew individually east to the Suffolk coast where we made our formation, with "E" in number 6 position, and set course for The Hague. From there we flew in formation over some of the major cities in the Netherlands including Arnhem. We all landed safely back at Graveley after four hours forty minutes.

We were later told that the Air Ministry was well pleased with the display, having received favourable comments from a number of sources. Our CO echoed that he was very pleased with the skill of the pilots.

On 7th May further formation practise with "E" in number 12 position. It lasted only 35 minutes for us as the Lanc became U/S and we returned to base on three engines.

On 8th May formation practise again, this time flying in "N" as "E" was under repair. One hour fifty minutes. I was Nav 1 on this and the previous flight.

On 9th May a further night cross-country with astro navigation as the main task. The pilot was "A" flight commander S/Ldr Mike Beetham in Lanc "A". We landed at 2am after a five hour flight.

On 10th May formation practise in number 6 position with me as Nav 1 for two hours. This time in "S".

On 21st May more formation practise in "Q" in number 6 position for one hour fifty minutes.

On 25th May a formation flypast over RAF Mildenhall and RAF Marham, two of the Command's main bases. I have no idea why this was made but it was possibly to show them what 35 Squadron could do. This time we were in "N" and it lasted almost two hours. It was taking a long time for "E" to be serviceable again.

On 27th May. Cross country training flight in "C" with the accent again on astro but with the Sun on this occasion. Also D.R. (Dead Reckoning) navigation.

It must have been at about this time that we were all called to the Briefing Room once again. Our CO was there flanked by the two Flight Commanders. Alan Craig said, "I am once again the bearer of good news. We have been invited to tour the United States and to take part in the American Air Forces

Day Flying Display at Long Beach airfield, Los Angeles, California on 1st August."

He went on to say, "I will read from the Movement Order, which I will intersperse with my own remarks". He then told us of the preparations that had already been made and how these would affect us.

"The operation will be officially known as "Operation Lancaster"

AIRCRAFT

We will be taking our sixteen Lanc FE1s, flying in displays in our established pattern of twelve with the remaining four as spares. Apart from formation displays, all flights will be made on an individual basis.

An Avro York will be with us, carrying some personnel and a selection of spare parts for our Lancs, which are impractical for us to carry. It will also be used to fetch spares which, hopefully, are unlikely to be needed, for example, a replacement engine.

PERSONNEL

The Graveley Station Commander, Group Captain RCM Collard DSO, DFC will be in command of the operation, with W/Cdr Alan Craig DSO, DFC in charge of flying with S/Ldr Michael Beetham DFC as A Flight Commander and S/Leader T Harris DFC as B. Gp Capt Collard will be a passenger in the York.

We shall be taking our ground crews with five in each Lancaster. We shall make them as comfortable as possible. We shall therefore have eighty qualified men available to service the sixteen aircraft.

There will be some postings of personnel in and out from the Squadron. It will be impracticable to take men whose demob numbers are programmed to come up whilst we are away and there may be other reasons for postings.

PAY

The Air Ministry has been apprised of the view that whilst we will be well looked after by the American Army Air Corps we will undoubtedly have to put our hands in our pockets at times. The Ministry has therefore decided that our pay will be doubled whilst we are away. This, presumably, will be from the time we leave these shores until we return but that has yet to be confirmed.

UNIFORM

All aircrew will be issued with a silver grey lightweight flying suit with the Squadron badge on the left breast. Ground crew will have white overalls. The flying suits and the overalls are intended for ceremonial occasions and will mostly be worn when we land at an American base where there will be a reception committee.

When we leave Graveley we will be wearing our normal working clothes. We will take with us our best blue.

The weather in places will be hot and it has been decided that all personnel will be issued with a tropical suit of jacket and trousers. Tailors with visit Graveley in a few days' time to take measurements.

All personnel will be issued with a spacious valise in which to put the clothes that we are not wearing. All of you must take the utmost care of your uniforms, etc, as obtaining replacements will be difficult to say the least.

At no time whilst we are away will civvies be permitted to be worn.

ROUTE

We will fly first to RAF St Mawgan, Cornwall, the RAF's most westerly base.

Our range, with full tanks, will not be sufficient for us to reach the eastern Canadian seaboard, and we shall have to refuel en route. The choice is limited and has fallen on Lagens in the Azores. Lagens is a small US Air Force base and does not have the facilities to accommodate an additional two hundred men. To overcome this problem it has been decided that A flight will leave St Mawgan on day one and, subject to the weather, will exit Lagens on day two. A signal will then be sent to St Mawgan and, again depending on the weather, B flight will take off for the Azores.

It will be appreciated, especially by the navs, that we will lose the benefit of Gee about four hundred miles into the route. We will then have to rely upon DR navigation, radio fixes, drifts off the sea and astro, so it will be back to the days of our training. H2S will, of course, be useless over the north Atlantic but it may help when we strike landfall. It will now become clear why there has been an accent on astro navigation on our recent training flights.

A flight will fly from Lagens to RCAF Gander in Newfoundland and, if things work out as planned, will be joined there by B flight the following day, After the sixteen aircraft have been serviced the sixteen will fly individually from Gander to Mitchell Field, New York.

This will be sufficient route information for the present.

We will leave Graveley on July 8th and fly in formation to St Mawgan from which A flight will depart for Lagens the following day. As plans stand at the present we are due back at Graveley on August 29th.

I am sure you all appreciate what a wonderful opportunity has been laid before us and how privileged we are to represent the RAF and our country on Operation Lancaster. We go as ambassadors and it behoves us all to act as such.

We may have visits from The Chief of the Air Staff and the Air Officer Commanding Bomber Command before we leave Graveley.

Between now and July 8th we will continue with our training mindful that on June 8th we will be leading the Victory Flypast over London.

Finally, I hope it will be possible for you all to have a short spell of leave before the end of June."

On May 28th we had formation practise in 'F' for the London Flypast lasting one hour thirty minutes.

On May 30th a short air test in 'E' followed on May 31 by an astro and DR cross country in "Q" lasting two hours.

On June 6th a second and final practise for the London Formation Flypast; this time the agreed route with the ETA over Buckingham Palace at 1300 hours precisely, as it would be on the day. We took off at midday in "E" and I see that for the first time with this aircraft I have noted the manufacturer's number, TW879.

We flew almost due east to the Suffolk coast, where we made our formation as we flew down that coast and then that of Essex. At Southend we turned to starboard and followed the line of the Thames to a point where we inclined to starboard to line up with Admiralty Arch, over which we would fly, and then The Mall, to bring ourselves over The Palace at the appointed time.

All went well without a hitch, including the ETA right on time. When we landed back at base there was a congratulatory message from the Ministry.

That night we took off at 1900 hours for a night cross country to practise astro and DR. I have no record of the route we followed but it must have been well over one thousand miles as we were airborne for seven hours in our faithful "E". We were all tired, Gill especially so, after keeping station in formation and then flying E seven hours in the dark.

On June 8th it was The London Victory Flypast. Unfortunately the weather was poor and it must have been touch and go whether the flypast would go ahead. Most of our formation aircrew were not privy to the precise details; we only knew that our twelve would lead the display. We afterwards learnt that because the cloud base was so low the plan for the faster aircraft to overtake the slower after The Palace did not work out as had been planned and there were problems. The flight controllers were having to cope with over three hundred aircraft! However, so far as we were concerned we had no problems and all went well including the most important part, being over The Palace right on the dot. We again had a congratulatory message from The Ministry with the accent on success in difficult conditions.

On June 17th and 19th we flew formation practises in 'E'. These would be the final practise flights before we flew to the American continent.

There had been one unhappy episode during the preparations for the trip. The man-made material for the uniform for use when it became too hot for best blue creased so easily that it looked quite dreadful. It was too late for some sort of replacement. Officers who had approved tropical uniforms would be allowed to wear them as would the few ground crew who had that kit. The remainder would have to wear the issue and resort frequently to the iron.

◆ ◆ ◆

35 Squadron Lancasters in formation over Nelson's Column during the Victory Flypast on 8th June 1946.

F/O Gill Hampson (3ʳᵈ from left) with his crew at Lagens, Azores.

35 Squadron Lancasters over East River, New York.

~ CHAPTER XIX ~

Operation Lancaster/Goodwill
8th July to 29th August 1946

O n July 8th we left Graveley at 1100 hours in our faithful "E", having flown an air test a few days previously. We flew in formation in our normal position, 6, and landed at St Mawgan after a flight of one hour forty minutes.

There were not many personnel left at Graveley but there was a good turn out from those who were there to wave us off. One of the WAAF officers took her camera and lay down on the runway at the take-off end to photograph the Lancs as they took off. It was a dangerous and rather foolhardy thing to do, she could have been killed, but she did get some marvellous pictures!

The weather was glorious and some of us went for a swim off the beach at St Mawgan, the first of many dips we were to have in the following seven weeks.

On July 9th 1100 hours saw us take off for Lagens. Our track was approximately 225 degrees so Nav 1 gave Gill the appropriate course to allow for the wind. I produced Gee fixes for a couple of hours to keep us on track. After that it was radio fixes from our Wireless Op. I experimented with the astrograph but that was not really necessary. To be honest, the weather was so much in our favour and the navigation aids so good, that we had no difficulty in locating Lagens after a flight of six hours forty five minutes. The other seven aircraft of A flight also landed safely although, for some reason, one had only a few minutes' worth fuel left!

We had time for a swim in the late afternoon and after the evening meal it was time for bed. The yanks showed their renowned hospitality and made us feel really welcome.

On July 10th at 0340 hours we set off for Gander in Newfoundland. Once again our track was a straight line, this time around 315 degrees but, of course, there was no Gee to start with and we had to rely on DR, but once again the radio fixes were good and kept us on track. I used the astrograph and took drifts off the sea and we were helped by the glorious weather. However, we had a long flight in front of us and weather can and does change. We were two hours thirty minutes into our journey when we were recalled to Lagens. Gander was fogbound and there was no alternative airfield within our range.

No doubt there was a sufficient backup to ensure that we all received that message because had we not then the affected aircraft would eventually have had to ditch!

The best laid plans of mice and men then went awry. B flight had received the message that A flight was on its way to Gander and consequently they had left St Mawgan.

The upshot of this was that both flights reached Lagens at around the same time! What the Air Ministry had carefully planned to avoid had, in fact, happened. The Yanks now were faced with the problem of coping with around two hundred men at the same time. Our hosts were magnificent; they pulled out all the stops to ensure we were well looked after. Gander remained fogbound the following day, so our hosts had to cope with their unexpected guests for nearly two days.

July 12th was, to start with, a repeat of the early part of July 10th but this time A flight landed safely at Gander after a flight of six hours 45 minutes, in daylight. All B flight also reached there safely.

We spent five days at Gander whilst the aircraft were serviced. The airfield had been built during the war by The RCAF as a base from which aircraft made in Canada or the US took off to fly to the UK. It was many miles from civilisation. I found it rather beautiful. It was surrounded by trees, vegetation, streams and small rivers and was very peaceful when aircraft engines weren't running! I doubt that my feelings would be shared by anyone who was stationed there for any length of time, however.

On July 17th at 0940 we took off for Mitchel Field, New York. It was a pretty straightforward flight with the aid of radio fixes and H2S was a help. We all landed safely after a flight of six hours twenty minutes. We then had to quickly don our flying suits and white overalls. The pilots had to line up the Lancs in formation flight sequence but in line abreast, facing the Control Tower. That was a magnificent sight for the photographers; sixteen white Lancs in a perfect line abreast. Alan Craig was greeted by the Air Force Base commander and everything went well. It was a good start.

In the evening there was a reception for the officers in the Officers' Mess. Certain dignitaries and officer's wives and girlfriends had been invited. It was a very friendly and happy evening. My abiding memory is of an officer's wife approaching and saying "Please say something, we love to hear you talk!"

On July 18th we performed a formation flypast over New York lasting one hour twenty minutes. How true this is I don't know but it was said that a suitable map of New York could not be found and Alan's crew had to navigate with the use of a road map. On this occasion we really had no choice but to follow the leader!

That evening Pete, our Wireless Op, said to me, "Let's go, with Robin, to the Waldorf Astoria in the town. I have wanted to do this for some time." We grabbed a cab, off base, and were soon there. Sitting at one of the bars we were approached by a quintessential Englishman in his tweeds and brogues who enquired what were three RAF officers doing in the Waldorf Astoria. I think it was Pete who facetiously said, "Having a drink." I went on to say that we were from 35 Squadron RAF which had been invited to take part in the US Army Air Force Day Flying Display at Los Angeles in August. We spent a few minutes talking generally and he then said. "When you come back to New York give me a ring and I will be pleased to take you out for dinner". He gave me his card. I thanked him and said we would do that.

On July 21st after three lively and interesting days in New York we left Mitchel Field at 1000 hours bound for Scott Field, St Louis, Missouri. The weather was bad and there was a great deal of turbulence but we landed safely after a flight of six hours.

It was to become evident that the people of St Louis had gone to a great deal of trouble to ensure that we would have a memorable visit to their famous city. We were to be there for three days after the day of arrival. A committee of The St Louis Chapter of The Red Cross had prepared a program for our officers for the first day. They had adopted the title Operation Goodwill instead of Lancaster. On Monday July 22nd from 2 til 5 pm we were to have a sightseeing tour of St Louis. Thirty of our senior officers were to attend a Reception and Tea from 5 to 8pm, hosted by the British Consul. Forty junior officers were invited to swimming and a buffet supper at "Vouziers", a mansion where we to be in the care of another Committee, also with the title Operation Goodwill. This would be from 5 to 8pm after which we would visit The Municipal Opera for a performance of *East Wind*.

I have no record of what happened the following day but no doubt the fine hospitality continued.

On July 24th the officers were driven to a mansion on the other side of St Louis, about forty miles distant from Scott Field, where there was to be a Special Reception and Ball to mark our visit. Our hosts had felt that we would probably be tired after the festivities and arranged for us to be flown in Dakotas from Lambert Field, close to where we were entertained, back to Scott Field. My log book shows take off at 0230 hours for a twenty minute flight!

On July 25th after a short night's sleep we took off from Scott Field at 10.30 hours en route to our next destination, Lowry Field, Denver, Colorado. The pilots had been warned that as Lowry field was 4,000 feet above sea level the air would be rarefied and landings and take offs would require more runway. We had no problem and landed safely after an uneventful flight of five hours ten minutes. At the beginning we had made formation and flown as such over St Louis and Kansas City.

We had no idea what awaited us at this Base, only that we could be sure of more outstanding hospitality. After our experience the previous day we hoped that we would sometimes be able to enjoy a normal night's sleep!

Another warm welcome awaited us. Lowry Field was a base of The American Air Force (AAF) Training Command. There was a Guard of Honour of one hundred officers and men for the welcoming ceremonies for which our aircraft were lined up as previously. We were each handed a booklet describing the history of the Base and a directory so that we could find our way around. We were also given a four page leaflet produced by The Denver Tramway Corporation entitled "Read as you go". This edition featured an article on the new Trolleys which had an automatic step in the doorway, controlling the doors. Up to date technology in 1946!

On July 26th we were to attend a reception in the Library of the Denver University Campus which would be hosted by the Chancellor and his lady. We were told that the entertainment during our stay in Denver had been organised by The English Speaking Union and The British Consulate.

On July 27th in the afternoon from 1 until 6 pm there was to be an "Open Day" at the Base. Examples of their Command's aircraft would be on display, together with our Lancs. We were asked to mingle with the crowds and, hopefully, answer any questions they may have about our aircraft and possibly what life was now like in the UK.

We had been well looked after during our stay at Lowry Field and would leave with happy memories.

On July 28th we were due to depart Lowry Field. We were looking forward to flying over The Rockies and The Grand Canyon, but it was not to be. The weather was bad with rain and low cloud. The American officers controlling this stage of the tour decided that we would all be a great deal safer in the circumstances if we were to fly on a Beam. This procedure involved the transmission of a radio beam which would be picked up by our wireless equipment from which the skipper and the crew would hear a constant note over their headphones. If the plane veered off to one side of track the note would change to a series of dots gradually increasing in volume. Veering to the other side would pick up a series of dashes. This system was new to most of us. We took off at 0935 hours and had no sight of anything but cloud until we sighted Long Beach Field, Los Angeles, California, five hours and thirty five minutes later! The Beam and our Skippers had been a good combination.

For the reception, on this occasion, the Lancs were lined up in flight formation in front of the Control Tower with Alan Craig's number 1 on its own at the front. The air and ground crews resplendent in their formal flying suits and white overalls, respectively, were in three rows in front of number 1.

The following day a reporter of *The Los Angeles Times* wrote: *"Although the war is over RAF personnel still stamp their feet smartly on parade"*.

We had made an impression!

The Reception was attended by a number of VIPs. Among these was Air Marshal Sir Norman Bottomley, Commander in Chief, Bomber Command, Air Commodore Frank Whittle, inventor of the Jet engine, AAF Top Brass, including The Base Commander, The British Consul General, and Sir C Aubrey Smith, accompanied by Nigel Bruce and his daughter Pauline, Richard Green and Peter Lawford representing the expats in the film industry. It was obviously an important occasion.

That evening there was a further reception in The Officers' Mess where we met AAF Officers of most ranks who were anxious to have a chat with us. They made us most welcome.

At this point I will mention that the American Press generally, appeared amazed that Alan Craig was only 23 years old, a veteran bomber pilot and Master Bomber and the youngest Wing Commander in the RAF. This appeared often. However, there is little mention of his Flight Commanders, Mike Beetham and "Shorty" Harris, both 22 and distinguished bomber pilots and certainly among the youngest Squadron Leaders in the RAF.

On July 29th we were split into small parties to be entertained by hosts in their Hollywood homes. Pete and I were part of a small group of officers who were to be looked after by Pauline, the daughter of Nigel Bruce at his lovely house and gardens. Among his other roles Nigel took the part of Dr Watson in the Sherlock Holmes films. Pauline was a fine host. She went to so much trouble to ensure that we enjoyed ourselves, including spending a large part of our time in a magnificent swimming pool.

That evening Pete, Robin and I decided to sample one of the Hollywood restaurants. We went to Mike Lyman's Grill where, for example, a large tenderloin steak cost $2.85!

Until now, because of the problems associated with entertaining just over two hundred men, we had been split into small parties of officers and other parties of airmen. However, on July 30th we were taken en masse to The Metro Goldwyn Meyer (MGM) Film Studios where we were divided into mixed groups of nine or ten for a tour of the studios, followed by lunch.

What a fascinating day that proved to be!

We saw film sets where the shooting had finished, such as "Anna and the King of Siam", which was awaiting demolition. Our group was taken to the set where they were filming "I Wonder Who's Kissing Her Now?" and had a photograph taken with the male lead, Mark Stevens and June Allyson, his leading lady.

Before lunch I went to the loo and the chap standing next to me turned to me and said, "Say bud which set are you on?" Quite understandable, as there were so many actors milling

Merle Oberon with Sqn Ldr Mike Beetham and members of the Squadron.

The author next to Mark Stevens and his leading lady June Allyson on the set of 'I Wonder Who's Kissing Her Now?'

around in all sorts of costumes. He laughed when I explained who I was and why I was there.

It was a marvellous day and everyone was so kind.

In the evening the officers attended a reception which had been laid on by the Film Industry specifically for us to meet a number of stars. These included C Aubrey Smith, Richard Green and his wife, Merle Oberon, Lana Turner and Mary Pickford. There were a number of others and they all appeared to enjoy meeting us.

On July 31st we were given a tour of the Hollywood area and Pasadena, where most of the stars lived in eye-catching mansions. We visited Grauman's Chinese Theatre where, imprinted in the concrete of the entrance, are the footprints and handprints of many of the renowned of the motion picture industry. We saw The Rose Bowl, the famous palace of sport, The Palladium which we were told was a popular night spot of the youngsters, who were agile devotees of swing and jitterbugging, along with other landmarks of that famous area.

That evening Pete, Robin and I went to Earl Carroll's Night Club, where, according to the PR blurb, we would see the most beautiful girls in the world in *Extravaganza*. The show was spectacular and although the blurb was somewhat exaggerated, the girls were certainly very attractive. In our uniforms the three of us stood out and it was not long before the PR people appeared. They wanted to know where in the UK we came from and the name of our local papers. They took photographs of the three of us as a group and individually. It was, of course, good publicity for the Theatre that we had taken the time in the course of our visit to Los Angeles to see their show and later there was small piece in each of our local papers.

The author (right) with Pete and Robin at Earl Carroll's nightclub.

On August 1st came the culmination of Operation Lancaster, or as our hosts preferred, Operation Goodwill, and there certainly had been a great deal of that. Army Air Force Day was the 39th Anniversary of the US Air Force, which had grown from a one page memorandum in 1907.

We took off at 1245 hours for our formation flypast of Los Angeles. We were over the area for one hour twenty five minutes flying for most of the time at 2,000 feet.

After we had landed a few of our planes taxied to the area where we joined our hosts' aircraft which were to be open to the crowds that were expected.

The organisers were not disappointed. I think the publicity that there were to be Lancasters open for visitors to the base to climb aboard had attracted a number of people who

35 Squadron Lancs lined up for reception at Long Beach airfield.

The 'Snafu Maru'.

wanted to see what these Lancasters were really like in the flesh. We were pleased to mix with the crowds, show them our Lancs and explain how they operated and to answer their questions.

Later that day came the end of another satisfying experience.

For dinner that evening Pete, Robin and I went to The French Room of the Los Angeles Ambassador where there was such a menu that we were really spoilt for choice.

I should, perhaps, make it clear that we could always dine with our hosts but they understood that we wished to sample what was available to "the man in the street".

August 2nd was to be our final day in Los Angeles and it was decided that we would be able to do as we pleased, within reason. However, an invitation was extended to any of our officers, who were keen swimmers, to spend the day, or as much of it as we wished, on the *Snafu Maru*. This was best described as a luxury motor yacht which the Yanks had captured from the Japs during the war. I decided to accept the invitation. The boat was moored in the Marina and we were able to dive off and swim in the Pacific on what was a glorious day. It really was a fitting end to the wonderful time we had experienced at Long Beach and Los Angeles in general.

On August 3rd we took off at 0945 hours for our next stop, Kelly Field, San Antonio, Texas. We made formation somewhere en route and flew over Kelly Field in that mode to herald our arrival. The flight had taken six hours and twenty minutes.

During the past few days the weather had turned much warmer and Gill had found that the most comfortable dress during the flights had been a pair of shorts and a pyjama jacket. This necessitated a quick change once we had landed!

We were invited to a picnic that evening at Koehler Park. This had been organised by The British War Brides Society of San Antonio to honour the RAF veterans. There was a large crowd who seemed very glad to be able to talk to us and there were, of course a number of expat war brides.

From August 4th to 7th we were to spend four clear days at Kelly Field and, as had always been the case in the USA , we were well looked after and were most often on the go. We were invited to a number of parties. We were taken to famous landmarks including The Alamo, where we spent a while in the museum. We went to the Zoo and spent a day on a very large ranch. The one problem was the heat. During the day the temperature was around 101 degrees. My abiding memory is that at night we lay on our beds bathed in perspiration, the humidity was so high. We never did find out why there was no air conditioning in our quarters.

On one of the days our officers were loaned the wives of the AAF officers at the base, who took us on a shopping tour. That was a very kind gesture. I bought Barbara two dresses, a pair of shoes, a handbag and some other small items for her trousseau.

Before we left Los Angeles I read in the local press a report of our visit which said we had fifteen Lancasters. When we reached Kelly field I learnt that we had left one behind at Denver, where it was awaiting a replacement engine to be fetched from somewhere by the York.

On August 8th we left Kelly Field at 0740 hours, flying individually to Andrews Field, Washington DC. We were now on our way home. The flight lasted seven hours twenty five minutes and would prove to be the longest of this tour. We parked the aircraft on the ramp in front of the Control Tower, as usual. There was then a brief reception, followed by the evening meal at 1800 hours. Very wisely no entertainment had been laid on for the remainder of the day, as it had been rightly assumed that we would be tired after the long flight. We were to find that the programme for the five clear days that we were to be at Andrews Field had been well planned but was to be much more formal than had been the case up to then.

On August 9th in the morning we had a talk by Group Captain Collard. All sports facilities at The Base were made available to us. These ranged from the use of the gymnasium to golf and even included horse riding!

All RAF personnel attended a reception at The British Embassy from 1800 until 2000 hours. This was hosted by The British Ambassador, accompanied Air Chief Marshal Sir Guy Garrod. Many other dignitaries were there.

On August 10th we took off at 1030 hours, made our formation and flew over Atlantic City, Philadelphia, Baltimore, The White House and the State Capitol. The event had been well publicised and many hundreds of people would have been able to see the formation of our 12 Lancasters and hear the roar of their 48 Rolls Royce Merlins since we were flying at just two thousand feet.

That evening the officers and airmen were again split into two parties. The airmen were taken to Chesapeake Park where there was swimming, dancing and a picnic supper. The officers were invited to The Officers' Club where they were joined by the officers based at Andrews Field for a buffet dinner and dance.

On August 11th Sunday services were available at churches of the main denominations for those who wished to attend. In the afternoon there was an Open House at The Base for

The British Colony in Washington, where they would be able to inspect our Lancs and converse with us.

That evening, places had been reserved for RAF personnel on The Capitol steps for those who wished to attend The Army Air Force Band concert.

On August 12th after breakfast the airmen were taken on a tour of Washington. The officers went on an abbreviated trip as they had been invited to visit the famous Federal Bureau of Investigation (FBI). Our hosts appeared to have selected some of the most attractive secretaries to escort us and show us how The Bureau operated. Robin and I had the company of two charming girls.

Towards the end of the visit I took Robin to one side and said "How about us inviting them to have dinner with us this evening as an appreciation of the wonderful hospitality that we have experienced on this tour?" Robin readily agreed and, somewhat to our surprise, the girls said they would be delighted. I was to escort Iola Mae Nelson and Robin, Dorothy Dee Brillhart. We booked a table at The Starlight Roof of the Hotel Roger Smith, one of the most expensive restaurants in Washington. The girls were good company, the food and service excellent and we had a most enjoyable evening. It cost us a packet but we felt we had been able to give something back in return for the wonderful hospitality that we had received in the States. Needless to say, we behaved as officers and gentlemen should. I had noticed that the British film *The Way to the Stars* was showing at a local cinema under its American title *Johnny in The Clouds*. It starred Michael Redgrave, John Mills, Rosamund John and Basil Radford. It was most appropriate for 35 Squadron's visit as it featured a Bomber Squadron and the crews during the war. It had most probably been especially laid on.

I asked Iola if she would like to come with me to view it the following afternoon. She said she would love to. Robin and Dorothy were unable to come with us, as she was working.

August 13th was a free day to give us an opportunity to see some of the places in Washington which we had seen from the air, such as The White House. We were due to leave Andrews Field the next day after a memorable visit to that Base and Washington DC.

On August 14th we were bound for Westover Field in Holyoke, Massachusetts. Mitchell Field, New York, was well within our range from Washington but it had been decided that we would first go to Westover Field in order to make a formation flypast over Boston, where it was thought it would be much appreciated by that city's pro-British element. The flight from Washington had taken three hours thirty minutes.

For some reason the planned formation flypast did not take place. However, there is an entry in my log book dated August 16th which reads "1500 hours – Dakota (aircraft) – passenger – Boston and return – 1.40". I cannot remember what was the purpose of this trip as we did not land. It could have been due to the weather.

We were again well looked after at Westover Field but I have no recollection of what else happened in the three days that we were there.

On August 18th we took off at 0800 hours for our return visit to Mitchell Field. The short flight lasted two hours. We were due to spend three clear days there whilst the aircraft were serviced before our long flight home, much of it over the North Atlantic.

We put this time to good use, including contacting the English gentleman, who, as promised, took Pete, Robin and me to a top restaurant, where we had a lavish dinner. There was a sequel, of which more later.

On August 22nd our wonderful time in the USA had come to an end. We had been in that country for five weeks. We took off at 0800 hours in our faithful "E" and landed at Gander after a flight of five hours. We were due to depart for Lagens on August 24th after the ground staff had again checked the planes to ensure all was as it should be. The sixteen Lancs were now back together after the one with the replacement engine had caught us up.

On August 24th we left Gander at 2300 hours for Lagens, so the flight would be mostly at night. The navigation procedure was much as it had been on the inward flight but the night gave me the opportunity to practise with the astrograph shooting the stars. The weather was good, we had an uneventful flight and landed at Lagens after seven hours at night and one hour ten minutes of daylight. That had been my longest flight in a Lanc.

On the morning of August 25th we learnt of a dreadful accident at Gander the previous night. The last of our aircraft to take off, skippered by F/O Cheshire had encountered compass trouble and was recalled. As it landed it hit some people who were standing in a prohibited area and there were fatalities. It was a sad and unfortunate end to what had been a very successful tour, which had generated so much goodwill.

Cheshire and his crew were detained at Gander pending an enquiry. It was not until some weeks later that we heard that they had all been exonerated from blame as the four who were killed and the one who was injured were in a prohibited area. The Lancaster was so badly damaged that it was written off. It was all very sad.

We never heard how Cheshire and his crew returned to the UK as we never saw them again.

Soon after that news we took off at midday for St Mawgan and, after another uneventful flight of six hours twenty-five minutes, we landed safely. To our astonishment we were met by Customs Officers, who were very thorough in questioning us as to what we had brought back!

Operation Lancaster or, as the Yanks would have it, Operation Goodwill, had been a wonderful experience and a privileged opportunity of a lifetime. We had flown many thousands of miles and had been the recipients of over-whelming hospitality, warmth and interest.

The weather that late August was typical of the Cornish coast at that time of year, predominately sea mist. After a day's rest to allow 'B' flight to catch up with us, we were supposed to fly past in formation over the south coast towns and then over London to celebrate our tour of The States but, because of the weather, this was delayed for three days.

On August 29th we were at last cleared to go. The aircraft had been standing out in the damp and some of them were difficult to start. Our CO was becoming irate as he feared we would be late over London and we had never previously had that problem. Eventually all were started and at the time of our slot we taxied from our dispersal point on to the perimeter track. In those days, and it is probably still the case, the perimeter track at St Mawgan at one point runs along the cliff. As Gill went to turn to starboard on to the track he applied the brakes and nothing happened! He had the presence of mind to shout to the flight engineer (a qualified pilot) "Full power port engines!" and we swung round to starboard with our port wing tip a few feet from the cliff edge. We had had a fortunate escape. If this had happened when we were landing, which on our formation flights was at thirty second intervals, we would probably have hit number 5 and had number 7 run into the rear of us. We had to wait until the brakes were repaired and then made our way back to Graveley alone, but in time for the welcoming party. Sir Norman Bottomley and many other distinguished guests were present. There were a number of speeches which were very praiseworthy for the Squadron, and the Lancaster, which had once again demonstrated what a reliable aircraft it was.

So ended Operation Lancaster/Goodwill. The British Press had followed the operation very closely and there had been many reports and articles whilst we were away. There was considerable coverage the following day of the welcoming home party.

After the success of the tour we were delighted to learn that we had all been granted two weeks leave.

◆ ◆ ◆

The customised squadron badge that adorned our Operation Lancaster/ Goodwill flying suits.

~ CHAPTER XX ~

RAF Graveley and RAF Stradishall
30 August 1946 to 6 March 1947

On September 10th I was back from leave and under-taking an air test of 'E' following its service after the tour. Airborne for one hour.

On September 13th there was formation practise lasting one hour thirty five minutes in preparation for a London flypast the following day.

September 14th was the day of the Battle of Britain Commemoration Flypast over London. Squadron again was the leader, over Buckingham Palace spot on, as usual, at 1300 hours. A friend who was present on the ground at the time of the flypast said, "To see those twelve Lancasters in formation and to hear the roar of forty-eight Merlins at such a low level is a sight and sound I shall never forget!" That flypast would be 35 Squadron's final display as the Showpiece Squadron of the RAF.

For that flight, and on the practise flight the previous day, we were using 'B' SW 313. It was to be my last flight with Gill, with whom I had flown as Nav II for over one hundred and fifty hours. A modest man, a skilled pilot and a good companion, he was off to be demobbed and back to civvy street.

A lot was to happen on September 15th and the following three days. Alan Craig was whisked away and we had a new CO, Wing Commander John Thornton Chapple. I was told that he was a regular officer and had been shot down quite early in the war and had spent a long time incarcerated as a POW.

Our new CO sent for me. He told me that on the 18th the Squadron would move to RAF Stradishall in Suffolk. We would be more comfortable there as it was a peacetime permanent station, built in 1938.

He went on to say that the Ministry had decided that there would no longer be substantive adjutants on a squadron and a member of aircrew would be appointed to that role. He had the pleasure to inform me that he had appointed me. No doubt, because I had been the *ex officio* assistant, I was considered the most suitable for that position.

I was delighted to have been appointed Adjutant to one of the most prestigious squadrons in the RAF. I regarded it as a great honour. It was some recompense for the disappointment in missing out on promotion to flight lieutenant. During the war, on selection as a pilot officer, there was promotion to flying officer after six months satisfactory service, followed by promotion to flight lieutenant after a further eighteen months. I had been due to have my second ring on July 1st 1946 but time promotion had been stopped on June 30th. The reason for this was that as wartime officers were selected for a permanent commission they would almost always have to drop a rank and sometimes, exceptionally, two. However, those who missed time promotion were to be paid at the scale they would have achieved had that not happened, so this somewhat relieved the disappointment.

On the day after I was appointed Adjutant, I paid my first visit to Stradishall, using my motorbike for transport. Stradishall was so different from Graveley. The construction of the airfield and buildings had been completed about a year before war broke out in 1939. The officers were accommodated in the same building as the Mess, which was much more convenient than having to brave the elements when going from the hut, as had been the case at Graveley. I had a pleasant room to myself and a nice office. I organised a few things on my first visit and then returned to Graveley.

The following day one of the pilots asked me if I would drive his Triumph Speed Twin to our new base, as he had to fly one of the Lancasters. I readily accepted, as this was a bike I had always wanted. It was the model that the Metropolitan Police was using and was considered to be about the best bike on the market at that time. I got as far as Cambridge when one of the spark plugs failed, so the ride was not as enjoyable as it might have been. That ride had also taken me away from Graveley for the last time.

Things soon settled down at Stradishall and I coped with my new job. I got on well with our new CO. Because of his long time away he was completely out of touch and I was able to ease him in. It was he who almost begged me to apply for a permanent commission, saying that I was the type of officer that the Service would need in the postwar years. He would support my application and, with my record so far, he had little doubt that it would be granted. I also discussed this with Mike Beetham who, like me, had been studying to qualify as an accountant before we had volunteered for aircrew. He proposed to stay in and you will have read that he rose to become a Marshal of The Royal Air Force and Chief of The Air Staff some years later. Barbara and I chewed over what I should do. She would have made a very good officer's wife in the peacetime Service, but in the end I decided to go back to accountancy. I was ambitious and one of my principal considerations was because I was a navigator and not a pilot it would be the latter who would make the most progress. In fact, some navigators did later achieve Air rank.

I enjoyed my time as Adjutant, for it was he virtually ran the squadron as Chief Executive and P.A. to the C.O. I particularly enjoyed the infrequent formal parades when the senior NCO would hand the Squadron over to me and I would then march to the CO, salute and say, "Parade ready for your inspection, Sir". These parades were important as they helped to preserve discipline. The Cold War was in being and one of my principal tasks was to ensure that we had on call as many complete crews as was possible on standby, ready to operate at short notice. This was not easy as the demob system was proceeding and every week we would lose several personnel as their number came up. This entailed reshuffling crews and liaising with other squadrons to fill gaps where it was not possible from our own resources. This, of course, also applied to ground crew.

One minor problem was that I did not have a secretary. However, I was quite handy with a typewriter and was able to prepare the weekly crew lists and type short communications when necessary.

With my workload I had little time for flying but I did not want to have to give this up, particularly as it would have defeated the object of having an Adjutant as one of the aircrew. The following is a list of my further flights.

On September 21st in 'E' once again as Nav II to Flt/Lt Hardy, DFC, DFM on an air test for P.I.C.A.O. which, from memory, was the acronym for Provisional International Conference for Aviation Operation.

On September 22nd in 'E' with Flt/Lt Hardy again, giving a demonstration of H2S for P.I.C.A.O.

On September 28th, this time in 'N' as Nav II to Flt/Lt Greig on a further air test for P.I.C.A.O.

On October 10th an air test in 'O' as Nav II to Flt/Lt Dawson followed three hours later by a night cross-country.

On December 12th unusually as Nav I in 'F' skippered by Flt/Lt Clarine DFC, AFC. You will have read earlier of Ken Clarine, who had been awarded an immediate DFC for his airmanship just before the war ended. Shortly after that he again demonstrated his skill and courage and was awarded an immediate AFC! We had a flight of four hours forty minutes, disposing of more unarmed bombs in Operation Wastage.

On December 18th in 'D' this time, again as Nav I to Ken, on a night cross-country followed by circuits of base and landings.

On December 20th again in 'D' as Nav I to Ken. We were briefed to take a Wing Commander and his trunk to RAF Lyneham in Wiltshire, a base of Transport Command. When we landed there after a flight of fifty minutes 'D' suffered a negative earth and was declared U/S. I had visions of being stuck there for Christmas but fortunately someone at Stradishall decided to despatch Flt/Lt Pennington in 'F' to rescue us.

The weather that winter of 1946/7 was dreadful but on January 6th 1947 a break appeared and it was decided that it was suitable for Ken to fly a cross-country in TW647 (for some reason there is no code letter shown in my log book) with me as Nav I. We took off at 14.45 hours and headed north.

When we reached our operating height I found that we had a tail wind which appeared to be in the region of 150 knots. This meant that on turning back we would be making little progress over the ground. I told our skipper, who contacted Stradishall and was told to abort and return to base. No sooner had we turned on to the reciprocal heading than he was told that base had closed down because of a heavy snowstorm and we were to divert to Woodbridge. Skipper told me not to give him a course for Woodbridge because having regard to the severity of the storm and the direction from which it was coming, by the time we reached Woodbridge that too would be closed down and we would be diverted to the Continent, where we might be for days. Instead, we would fly the course we were on and he would have a go at getting into base. We were confronted with blinding snow but we managed to keep on track and reach Stradishall. Skipper had to abort his first attempt to land and went round again. At one point on the second attempt I heard the rear gunner say over the intercom, "This is getting a bit dicey Skipper, our wheels have made ruts in the snow over the roof of one of the hangars." As we turned to make a third attempt I could see that this was so. On that third attempt Ken brought us safely down on a runway covered in snow, a remarkable feat in those conditions and a demonstration of truly outstanding airmanship. I never heard whether he was finally given permission to land at base or whether he was reprimanded for disobeying orders – but the crew owed their lives to him.

There was some talk on the squadron that, notwithstanding his courage and skilful airmanship, Ken must have a jinx. There was always superstition on an operational squadron but up to that point I had not had much truck with it. However, on the few occasions I had flown with Ken, almost always something unusual had happened.

On January 9th the weather cleared and we set off again with Ken, this time in TW880 (which must have come off the production line immediately after 'E') with me again as Nav I on a cross-country. At our operating height, over the south of France, there was a loud bang and a vivid blue flash from the nose to the tail. We had been struck by lightning and were all rather shaken. Fortunately the trailing aerial was earthed, so I was told, and we appeared to have suffered no damage. We landed safely at base after a flight of three hours forty five minutes.

That was to prove to be my final flight in the RAF.

My log book for January was signed off by Mike Beetham, as it had been every month since December 1945. He was now OC Flying Flight but would leave Stradishall the following month to further his career in the RAF.

I made up my log book for the final time, to the end of February 1947:

Day	*396 hours*
Night	*94 hours*
Total	***490 hours***

Somewhat surprisingly, this comprised over two hundred take offs and landings.

I continued with my duties as Adjutant until I was demobbed.

There was one incident during that time which was the sequel to which I referred when writing about our second visit to New York. I was in my office one morning in January when a call came through from the Guard Room. There was a Squadron Leader from The Provost Marshal's Office who wished to see me and he would rather I went to The Guard Room than he came to my office. He produced an air letter which he handed to me and asked whether I had written it. It was my letter of thanks to the man who had taken us to dinner. I answered him in the affirmative and he then asked me a few questions, which boiled down to what we had told that man. He then said, "Your 'English gentleman' was, in fact, a colonel in the Russian KGB."

To say I was astonished is an understatement but the Squadron Leader appeared quite satisfied, we shook hands and he left.

I received my demob notice at the end of February. I was instructed to attend The RAF Dispersal Centre in Lancashire on March 6 and I would be demobbed the next day.

So my service in The Royal Air Force from October 1942 to March 1947 would come to an end. I had been exceptionally fortunate, since at most times I had been in the right place at the right time. I had mixed with men from many walks of life, made friends, and some of those friendships were to last a long time. I had met famous people and seen and done things that most people would not see or do in their lifetime. I had experienced some dangerous situations and had been fortunate to come through them unscathed.

One of my special memories would be of the camaraderie of the crews with whom I had flown, particularly with Gill. Each one of us was there for the others and we made a happy team.

So now it was time for me to go back to the firm that I had left in 1943, to study hard and qualify as an accountant.

But I would take two weeks away before then, as Barbara and I were due to be married at West Bridgford on 15th March.

◆ ◆ ◆